ENGLISH
FOR
SCAMMERS

Chuck Sandy
Dorothy Zemach

WAYZGOOSE PRESS

English for Scammers

Copyright © 2014 by Chuck Sandy and Dorothy Zemach

Published by Wayzgoose Press.

Edited by Dorothy E. Zemach.
Cover design and interior formatting by DJ Rogers.

First printing: UK, February 2014
Second printing: Worldwide, March 2014

ISBN-10: 1-938757-11-4
ISBN-13: 978-1-938757-11-2

TABLE OF CONTENTS

HOW TO USE THIS BOOK

This book is available both, as a paperback, and as an ebook in a variety of common file formats. It can be used in a business letter writing class or individually as a self-study guide.

We recommend going through the units in order, as each one builds on the previous topics and information.

Answers to the unit exercises and the final exam are available at the back of the book.

Note: Email addresses have been obscured; we didn't want to risk the chance of a scammer having used some innocent party's actual email address. Phone numbers have likewise been altered. Names remain as we received them.

ACKNOWLEDGMENTS

The authors wish to thank the following reviewers of this book in manuscript for their comments and suggestions:

- Nigel Caplan, University of Delaware, USA
- Mark R. Freiermuth, Gunma Prefectural Women's University, Japan
- Tammy LeRoi Gilbert, author, materials developer, and editor, USA
- Jason R. Levine, author and teacher trainer, USA
- Bill Spruiell, Professor of Linguistics, Central Michigan University, USA
- Shelly Sanchez Terrell, author and teacher trainer, USA
- Ken Wilson, author and teacher trainer, UK

FORMATTING

An email is not as formal as a business letter printed on paper, but it is more formal than a text message. People expect a serious, sincere email to conform to certain formatting conventions. If your email looks very different, people won't take it seriously; your message may even hurt potential business opportunities.

The Look of a Standard Email

1. Subject line

Choose the subject line of your email carefully. This is the place to identify the topic of your message – your reason for emailing. You don't need to write a complete sentence; if the title is too long, your recipient won't see it all in his or her mailbox at first glance anyway.

Even email programs with automatic spellcheckers sometimes don't check the titles, so be sure to read your title carefully to make sure you haven't omitted or repeated any words, and that all words are spelled correctly.

The abbreviation Re: means that what follows is "about that subject." It's used for replies only. If someone sends you an email titled *Interesting proposal*, when you write back you can use the title *Re: Interesting proposal*. Never use Re: for a first email contact. Most email programs will add the Re: automatically when you use the "reply" function.

Remember not to use your own name or the name of your recipient as your subject title. The email program will show those names automatically.

Examples of good email titles:

A business proposal

Would like to schedule an appointment

Application for arts grant

Notice that (unlike, say, for a book title) not all major words in the subject line are capitalized. You do not need final punctuation at the end of a phrase.

Examples of bad email titles (all taken, unchanged, from emails sent to us):

Hi

Loan Offer!!!

Re: Thank You

FBI Headquarters in Washington, D.C

Email subject lines should never be written entirely in capital letters. And they should never ever contain the entire message.

Figure 1: Email subject lines should certainly never contain the entire message and be written in all capital letters. (Yes, this was an actual subject line; not the body of the email!)

To:	John Doe@xxxxxx.com
From:	Jane Smith@xxxxxx.com
Subject:	MY NAME IS MS. CARMEN L LAPOINT. I AM THE HEAD OF UN UNDER-SECRETARY-GENERAL FOR INTERNAL OVERSIGHT SERVICES.THIS IS TO INFORM YOU THAT I CAME TO NIGERIA YESTERDAY FROM CANADA, AFTER SERIES OF COMPLAINT FROM THE FBI AND OTHER SECURITY AGENCIES FROM ASIA, EUROPE, SOUTH AERMCA AND THE USA RESPECTIVELY, AGAINST THE FEDERAL GOVERNMENT OF NIGERIA AND THE BRITISH GOVERNMENT FOR THE HIGH VOLUME OF FRAUDULENT ACTIVITIES GOING ON IN THESE TWO NATIONS.AS DIRECTED BY UN SECRETARY GENERAL MR BAN KI-MOON, WE ARE WORKING IN COLLABORATIONS WITH THE NIGERIAN EFCC AGENCIES AND WE HAVE DECIDED TO AUTHORIZE THE GOVERNMENT OF NIGERIA TO EFFECT YOUR OVERDUE PAYMENT WORTH $5.5M ONLY INTO YOUR ACCOUNT WITHOUT ANY FURTHER DELAY YOUR DETAILS INCLUDING YOUR NAME PHONE NUMBER AND YOUR ADDRESS FOR VERIFICATION AND IMMEDIATE PAYMENT

2. Font

Most email programs let you choose a font for sending messages. Use a common, standard font such as Arial, Verdana, Calibri, or Times New Roman, in size 10, 11, or 12. Black. This looks businesslike, and means that your message will be easy to read. Even if you choose a fancy font, your recipient's email might not show it correctly. This is another reason to use a typical font.

Italics and bold should be used rarely, or not at all, especially in short messages.

3. Format of the Body

You do not need to write the date and your address at the top of an email. The date will show up automatically in the receiver's email program; your name and address should appear at the bottom, in your signature block. Your email should have these sections:

Dear Ms. Zemach,	[salutation: see Unit 2]
I am writing to let you know that …	[body of the email – your message. See Unit 2]
Sincerely,	[closing: see Unit 2]
Chuck Sandy	[your full name]
~ ~ ~ ~ ~ ~ ~ ~ ~ ~ ~ ~ ~ ~ Chuck Sandy Job Title Company Name Company Address ~ ~ ~ ~ ~ ~ ~ ~ ~ ~ ~ ~	[signature block; this can also include your telephone number and Skype contact information. See Unit 2]

Do not center any of the text or "block justify" it (even margins on the right and left). Use ragged right margins.

Figure 2: ragged right margins

Skip a line between:

- the salutation and the first paragraph
- all of your body paragraphs
- your last paragraph and your closing
- your closing and your name (sometimes people delete the skipped line here, which is OK)
- your name and your signature block, if you have one

Because you are skipping lines between paragraphs, you do not need to indent each paragraph. Start every paragraph at the left margin. The salutation, closing, name, and signature block also begin on the left.

Figure 3: Breaking every rule at once: An email in bold, italic, Comic Sans font in three colors, centered, with no salutation. The sender doesn't seem like a diplomat; the sender seems like a clown.

Subject	Consignment
Sender	you@sitedemo.com
Recipient	me@sitedemo.com
Date	Today 11:35 AM PST

Attn Package Beneficiary:

I want to acknowledge you tha! t we have finally succeeded in getting your page worth's of 7.5million out of (ECOWAS) Economic Community of West African States department with the help of Mr. James George Attorney General of Federal High Court of Justice Benin Republic which act as your foreign Attorney representative here in Benin Republic.

Meanwhile every necessary arrangement has been made successfully with the Agent Jerry cook for the delivery of your Consignment Box and every Document guiding your delivery is well updated so you are advised to reconfirm full delivery information to the Agent Jerry cook right now as he is current at John F. Kennedy International Airport (JFK)new york with your Consignment Box. He has alre! ady called me with his number on his arrival 4hours ago.

He is waiting to hear from you today with the information, NOTE:The Diplomatic agent Jerry cook does not know that the content of the consignment box is $7.5Million and on no circumstances should you let him know the content. The consignments was moved from here as india Cloths, so never allow him to open the box on OK.

Figure 4: While it is a good idea to have left and right margins, there is no need to label left and right margins.

left
border

right
border

Hello,

You were recently chosen as a potential candidate to represent yoru professional community in the **2013 Edition of Global Who's Who.**

We are please to notify you that your candidacy was formally approved on April 1st, 2013. **Congratulations!**

The Publishing Committee selects you as a potential candidate, based upon your current standing as well as criteria from executive and professional rosters. Given your background, the Publishing Director believes your profile would make a fitting addition to our publication.

As we are working off of secondary sources, we must receive verification from you that your profile is accurate. After receiving verification, we will validate your online listing within 7 business days.

There is no fee or cost to be included.

To verify your profile and accept the candidacy, please click here.

Please kindly note that our registration deadline for this year's publication is **June 30th, 2013**. To ensure you are included, we must receive your verification on or before this date.

On behalf of our Committee I salute your achievements and welcome you to our association.

Sincerely yours,

John DAgostino
Registry Administrator

1. Look at the images of emails. Write three formatting mistakes made in each one. (There might be more than three; just choose your favorites!)

In class: compare your answers with a partner when you are finished.
Alone: Check your answers at the back of the book.

a.

> I am Mrs Rabakha Phillip i have a Foundation home,i have a deposit $37.8m got your mail in web search i hope you are honest believer in Christ get back to me.

b.

> I am Mr.Bright Kware General Accountant of Hang Seng Bank Ltd. I have a deceased client funs in my bank of $44.5 Million USD and i need you to front as beneficiary,your benefit is 50% of the total funds.If you are interested contact me for more information via:
>
> (mrsbitihtgkware@xxxxxxx.com)
>
> Sincerely
> Mr.Britght Kware

2. Think about why formatting is important. How does following the conventions help the reader of the email? How does it help the writer?

In class: Discuss your ideas in a group.
Alone: Take a few minutes to gather your thoughts, and then write your response for five minutes. You can type an electronic document or write on paper.

OPENINGS AND CLOSINGS

The beginning and the ending of your letter are important places to make a good impression. Begin correctly and you will inspire confidence right way; end correctly and you will leave a good impression.

OPENINGS

Almost everyone likes to receive personal letters and emails in which we are addressed by our correct name in an appropriate manner. This is even more important in business emails, however, since you are more likely to be writing to someone you don't know well. It is also important to make a good impression because you want something – you are trying to conduct business. Perhaps you want to buy something, or sell something, or complain about something, or even get a job. Being polite and appropriate is an important part of achieving your goals.

No one, though, likes to receive anything that makes it clear right from the start that the writer doesn't even know to whom he or she is writing – and hasn't tried very hard to find out.

Even if you have never met the person you're writing to before, try to find out the person's name. Check the organization website. If there's a phone number, call and ask ("Could you tell me the name of your Director of Marketing, please?"). If you absolutely cannot find a person's name, there are still some appropriate forms of address. But let's look at names first.

If you are writing to someone you don't know at all, you will almost always want to use that person's last name. (In English, the "last" name is the family name. In some cultures, this is written first, but in English, the "first" name is your given name. Your last name is the same thing as your surname or family name.)

You are likely to be writing to either a man or to a woman. Your choices are *Mr.* + *last name* for a man, and *Ms.* + *last name* for a woman. Remember that *Miss* is used only for young, single women, and *Mrs.* only for married women – whereas *Ms.* can be used for any woman. Therefore, Ms. is the sensible choice.

If you are writing to John Smith, a man, write

Dear Mr. Smith,

If you are writing to Jane Smith, a woman, write

Dear Ms. Smith,

If you are writing to Chris Smith, who could be either a man or a woman, write

Dear Chris Smith,

> Remember that in English, the family name, or surname, comes last. The given name comes first. So, *Chuck Sandy*; not *Sandy Chuck*.

In American English, these salutations are followed by a comma. In very formal letters, they may be followed by a colon.

Dear Ms. Smith:

In British English, there is no period used with Mr or Ms, and no comma after the salutation:

Dear Mr Smith

What happens when you ignore these conventions? Let's take a look.

Dear Friend,

How are you today? Hope all is well with you and your family? I hope…

A real friend would already know your name. Someone who doesn't know your name isn't a friend. Immediately, then, the receiver of this email is suspicious. Solicitous inquiries as to one's family's health don't help (in fact, they hurt – see Unit 7).

What's even scarier is when a writer from out-of-the-blue greets us with a term reserved for those most dear to us – yet does not seem to know our name at all:

> Dearest Be-love One,
>
> My decision to contact you today is because I got a reference about you from a friend when I was sharing my opinion…

Besides, the correct term is *Dearest beloved one*, not *Dearest Be-Love One*. (And such a phrase would only be used romantically, not in a business letter.) Given the inappropriate use of that term made even worse with spelling and punctuation mistakes, that's a letter few will finish reading.

That's bad enough, but then there are those writers who don't even mention friendship, possible love, or any implied relationship at all… and just begin with a shout.

> Hey there!
>
> I don't know reasons to I don't see virtually any comments on your side. Might be some thing is wrong with private email address. If you wanna do business, I'm gonna need...

That sort of *Hey there* might be all right for an SMS or a personal message on Facebook, when it's usually clear that we do know the writer, but never ever for an email which goes on to discuss the possibility of doing business. If you wouldn't walk into a corporate head office for the first time, throw open the CEO's door, and call out *Hey there!*, don't do it in a business email either.

Could anything be worse than being addressed and greeted in these impersonal yet oddly familiar ways? Yes. Receiving a mail in which someone addresses you by a name you are never called, and in which you are greeted with a *Salute!* might be worse.

> Salute, Charles Sandy!
>
> Huh, you have been disturbed by Tim Stites, Three days ago I have payed attention to your profile on Facebook.

No one calls Chuck Sandy "Charles" except his mother when she's upset with him.

And no one ever addresses him by only his family name, like this:

> Dear Sandy,
> I write today to give you news about our newest product.

If you cannot tell which is a person's first name and which is the last name, then use both. Don't just blindly guess. However, a little research (and some checking on the Internet) can usually help you figure out which name is the person's last name.

Even worse is receiving an email that seems like it is not for you at all:

> My dear Salvador
>
> Tenderness which becomes at times almost insupportable for those in love. But everyone needs it, agree?

Who is this Salvador? Anyone not named Salvador would stop reading at this point, and certainly would not agree with the statement being made... or click on any included link.

If you do not know the name of the person to whom you are writing and it is impossible to discover it, it is permissible to begin with *To Whom It May Concern*, especially if you are writing to get information or settle a claim. (In British English, use *Dear Sir or Madam*).

> To Whom It May Concern:
>
> I recently purchased an ebook reader from your company, but did not receive a user manual. As I am unable to find the manual online, could you please let me know where I could locate this or else send me a copy? Thank you very much.
>
> Sincerely,
> Michael Dupont

Notice how the writer gets right to the point after the salutation *To Whom It May Concern*. He does not offer a greeting such as *Hello!* or *Salute!* Such a greeting would be inappropriate. Likewise, Michael does not ask about the health or well-being of the person who will read this letter because he only has a business relationship with the company where the reader works. They are not friends and (probably) never will be.

You may also use a job title, if that is all you can find – although a name is still the first choice.

Dear Marketing Director,

Dear Admissions Officer,

But please – only use "Dear." Not *Hi Marketing Director!* Not *Hey there, Marketing Director!* And certainly never *Salute, Marketing Director!*

CLOSINGS

After your final paragraph, you will end your email with one of these phrases:

Sincerely, (British English: Yours sincerely)

Best regards,

Best wishes,

and then "sign" your name by typing your first and last name (with no title like Mr. – titles are used to address other people, not to refer to yourself). However, if the person you are writing to might not be able to tell whether you are a man or a woman from your name, it is acceptable to add a title afterwards to let them know:

Best wishes,

Dorothy Zemach (Ms.)

It doesn't matter whether you use *Sincerely* or *Best wishes*, so just choose your favorite one and use it every time. But you must have some type of business-like closing that includes your name. To not do so make your letter seem unprofessional.

Often, business people use a "signature file", which appears below their signed name, that gives their job title, company name, mailing address and other contact information, such as telephone number or Skype name. If your signature file includes your full first and last name, you can leave your last name off your signature, although this is less formal.

I look forward to seeing you soon.

Best wishes,
Chuck

Chuck Sandy
author, teacher trainer, and motivational speaker
Aichi, Japan
Skype: charnelsan

It is not necessary to include your email address in your signature file because once your message has been received, the receiver knows your email address.

None of these closings is correct:

Regards,
MRS,GRACE

Please reply if interested via this email.Mrs.Gina.Rinehart@qq.com

God Bless You.

Best regards,
Mr. Brian Hanselman.
STORAGE OFFICER Terminal 5 Extension 11
Phone: 555-444-6657
Email: secmkoo@xxxxxx.ca

Regards,
David Wu
EIHHZLQIVKOCURVEBFOCIMOHELHXKYDCIBOUJG

Thanks,
Shilpi
Developer@Intel

Notice how the writer of this letter begins with a proper salutation, quickly establishes a connection to the receiver, and then gets right to the point in a professional yet friendly manner:

Dear Mr. Sandy,

I hope all is well with you. I'm using one of your books in my class and follow your posts on Facebook. I'm hoping you would consider helping me with a research project I am doing. It would only take a few minutes of your time. If you have time, would you mind completing a survey I am doing for my class? If so, please let me know and I will send you a link to the survey.

Sincerely,

Fatima Bazoli

That is a letter that is likely to get a response… and did.

WALL OF SHAME

From: Bigguy <suppamalo@xxxxxx.com>
Date: Sun, Feb 2, 2014 at 5:18 PM
Subject: from Elena
To: Postmaster <big64guy@xxxxxx.com>, Administrator <kieracarson@xxxxxx.com>

Hello!!! I don't know as to commence because it is my first-ever practice of knowledge in the Internet. But I write you this writing that will get become acquainted with you. I didn't get pick up on the Internet ne'er and so I don't know what to write. But I will to tell that I was tired of loneliness and I wish to find the love and to start the serious relations. And I will be glad if you write to me and you will choose to get acquainted with me. I don't know why I write to you, but in you there is something like that attracts me. I won't write about myself much, whether because I don't know you will become interested in acquaintance to me. But after all it is the Internet and if you don't write to me, I will understand you. But I will trust that I will find your writing and I will write to you more about myself in the next letter. And now, I will write about myself tersely. My name is Oleshka. And I am from Russian Federation. I am 30 years old. If you desire to hear about me better, write to me about yourself in larger detail. But I want to tell you at once that I treat familiarity very seriously and I will from you same. Because I heard that on the Internet there are people who compose for entertainment cheerfully to spend time and to whom money is necessary. And me it doesn't interest. But it seems to me that you are very serious man and I choose like to know you larger. Surely I may be mistaken but if we know each other better, time will show all. Do you agree? For me it is the opening step and it very laborious, but I trow in the best and the next ensuing step for you. I will wait very much for your answer. Olenka.

Unit 2 Exercises

Work alone. Correct the openings, closings, and other mistake in these letters. Remember to consider information you learned in Unit 1.

1. You are writing to someone named Lex Umbro in order to introduce a new website, which you are hoping he will use.

> Hi!!! Lex!
>
> This is our newest singles site.
>
> Check it out!!!
>
> Ludmila, Elena...

2. You are writing to Chuck Sandy, hoping that he will answer a question. You do not know Chuck well at all, but you follow his posts on Facebook and have heard him speak at a conference.

> HALLO Mr CHACK SUNDAY,
>
> PLEASE IF YOU CAN TELL ME THE LINK WHERE I CAN FIND OUT ABOUT MOTIVATION. I BEG YOU, SIR. I AM DESPARATELY.
>
> ADI

3. You are writing to a company about a bill you received. You do not know the name of the person you are writing to but have an email address for the customer service department.

> Hey there!
>
> I hope you are fine. There is a mistake in my bill. I attach a copy.
>
> Please correct this at once.
>
> Have a nice day! ☺
>
> Jennifer Lorant

4. You are (so you claim) Ambassador Terrence McCuley. You are concluding a letter to ask that someone write you back before Thursday. End the email with an appropriate closing and signature file (you will have to invent some information).

MY FLIGHT IS THURSDAY AND I EXPECT YOU TO COMPLY BEFORE THEN SO THAT THE DELIVERY CAN BE COMPLETED. IF YOU DO NOT COMPLY,

THEN IT WILL NOT BE MY FAULT IF YOU DO NOT RECEIVE YOUR PACKAGE EMAIL ME AT U.S AMBASSADOR TO NIGERIA

AMBASSADOR TERRENCE MCCULEY

EMAAIL----{terrence.mcculey4@xxxxxx.com}

PHONE: +234-81850-97788

---

5. Think of a friend or teacher's name to use for the opening. Use your own information for the closing. You may make any other changes you wish to the body of the letter (although more information about body paragraphs will be covered in future units).

Dear Valued Customer!!!,
We have concluded to effect your payment of $3.7Million, through western union, but the maximum amount you will be receiving each day starting from today is $5,000.00 daily until the funds is completely transferred.
Kindly Contact Dr.Douglas Hall,TEL: +555 99 61 36 35
E-mail:(douglashall2006@xxxxxx.in.th)

Though, Dr.Douglas Hall, sent $5,000.00 in your name today so contact Dr.Douglas Hall, or you call him as soon as you receive this email and tell him to give you the Mtcn, sender name and question/answer to pick the $5,000.00 Pls let me know as soon as you received all your funds $3.7Million,
Thank you

Check your answers at the back of the book.

From: Dr.Fabietti Massimo <officefile2253@xxxxxx.net>
Date: Mon, Feb 10, 2014 at 2:42 AM
Subject: Complement;
To: nfstrickland@xxxxxx.com

Complement;

I write to inform you that our delivery agent is currently at St Louise International Airport Montana more than 3days ago,
His Name is Diplomat John Magabush. He arrived with your consignment package which contain $18.2MUSD

Please Email Him your Full home address, nearest airport, And Mobile Number on how to reach to your Door Step including your Identity Proof.
That will help him for smooth delivery Note.

Don't let him know the content because it contains $18.2MUSD His contact E-mail (jmagabush@yahoo.fr)
Dr.Fabietti.Massimo
Tel: +555 68654433
DHL DIRECTOR

From: Mr.Mike Wensman <mariangela.delussu@xxxxxx.it>
Date: Wed, Feb 5, 2014 at 1:48 AM
Subject: From Western Union Branch Cotonou
To:

I'm An Assistant Manager Western Union Branch Cotonou (Bank of Africa Benin SA) Benin Republic, My Name Is Mr.Mike Wensman, I am responding back to you thismorning to inform you that Our General manager just passed away 5days ago (((Died)))luckily i went through all the files and found out that you have incomplete transfer in our custody Therefore re-confirm your current address Full name, Phone number, Address to our office I need your urgent respond today so that we shall finalize the transfer of your $950.000.00.Thanks

---

From: Michael Smith <officemail.01@xxxxxx.net>
Date: Wed, Feb 5, 2014 at 5:42 PM
Subject: Re: Waiting for your urgent respond.
To:

Good Day
Compliment of the season.
I know that as you read this email, it will come to you as surprise and a lot will go through your mind because we have not met or seen each other before but i want you to know that this email is for you as i have thefeeling that we are meant to do this together. Let me introduce myself, my name is Michael Smith and I want you to assist me received huge sum of (Ten Million Five Hundred Thousand United States Dollars) for Investment purpose in your country and am willing to offer you 40% of the total sum for your great support. You might also wonder how i got your contact, I got it through the internet when i was looking for a trust worthy person i can trust to handle this project. This offer is 100% genuine and risk free. kindly indicate your interest by given me your direct Cell Phone Number and any identification of yourself send to officemail.03@ xxxxxx.net (Mike Smith).

PUNCTUATION AND CAPITALIZATION

Although some think that punctuation is not very important, sometimes it is a matter of life and death – as in this famous example that has been making its way around the Internet for a long while:

Let's eat, Grandma!

Let's eat Grandma!

In the first sentence, the writer is calling Grandma to dinner or suggesting they go out together to get something to eat. However, the second sentence without a comma is suggesting that Grandma *is* dinner.

Punctuation

Commas and other punctuation marks are important, although some writers seem to put them everywhere, as in this example from a writer who calls herself Tanya:

---

dearest beloved,

How are you? i hope, all is ok! My name, is tanya, from a small Village near tirana, albania I\'m a rather shy girl at first. i open up a little more, as i get to know someone. i attache my Foto. i hope you liked it. i am a not a clever girl but I am kind. I like, craftwork, baking, sewing and so on. i do many things to make myself HAPPY for example, playing piano, DANCING to music, doing aerobics and listening to STORIES. i am looking for a strong decent man. i do not know what to write because i never used the Internet for acquaintance before. Write to ME if you want to, learn more about me; And see my other pictures. i will, WAIT YOUR LETTER. Write to me soon, i will send another FOTO.

take Care!

tanya

Ps: there is the chance, We can do the business, also.

In addition to starting off her letter with an inappropriate salutation and greeting, in which she doesn't even capitalize the first letter in *Dearest beloved*, Tanya goes on to commit a punctuation crime with all of her commas, sentence fragments, capitalization errors… and what is that semi-colon doing there?

Tanya has seven unnecessary commas in her letter. Can you find them? Then there is a whole sentence that should have commas but doesn't. Did you find that? Also, what punctuation should Tanya have used instead of that semicolon [;] she uses? Just think about this for now. You'll have a chance to correct all of her mistakes in the exercise section at the end of this unit.

Clearly, though, Tanya's letter loses effectiveness because of her errors. Very few people would want to meet someone who makes so many mistakes in an opening letter. Likewise, this would not be the kind of person you'd wish to do business with.

Start each sentence with a **capital letter.** End each sentence with a **period** [.] or **question mark** [?]. (In informal emails, people sometimes end sentences with an **exclamation mark** [!], but you won't need any in your first business email). This rule sounds simple, but writers still struggle with it, like this one:

> This is to bring to your notice that because of the impossibility of your fund transfer through the western union network, we have credited your total sum of $2.5millon valid fund into an ATM MASTER CARD and I have paid the re-activation fee and the delivery of the ATM Card To you, I paid it because the ATM Card worth of $2,500,000.00 which I have registered for delivery yesterday has less than 16 days to expire in the custody of the FedEx Company and when it expires, the money will go into Federal Government treasury account.

How many sentences is that? It's punctuated as just one, but it should be … two? three? It's very hard to tell. The lack of separate sentences makes the whole message confusing!

Commas are tricky, but their usage is governed by grammar rules that can be learned. Good writers learn the rules. Poor writers put commas wherever they feel like it and leave them out of the places where they're needed. Don't be one of those writers.

This book cannot cover every aspect of comma usage in English, but here are three common rules you should learn to begin with:

1. Use commas to separate items in a sequence – including the last item.

   I like craftwork, baking, sewing, and so on.

2. Use commas before *but, and, so, and,* and *yet* to separate two independent clauses (groups of words that have a subject and a verb).

   I am not a clever girl, but I am kind.

3. Use a comma to separate coordinate adjectives – that is, adjectives of the same type, such as two different words that give a value judgment. Adjectives of different types (such as age, size, and color) are not separated by commas.

   I am looking for a strong, decent man.

   She's a beautiful young child.

Semicolons can be trickier than commas. Fortunately, they are not very common, and even good writers sometimes avoid them. You can, too; but just in case you'd like to use one, here are some rules you should follow.

1. Use a semicolon instead of a period to separate two sentences or to avoid using a conjunction to string them together.

> Write to me soon; I will send another photo.

2. You can use a semicolon before words and expressions like *however*, *for example*, and *therefore* when they introduce a list following an independent clause or when such words are used between two independent clauses.

> I do many things to make myself happy; for example, playing the piano, dancing to music, doing aerobics, and listening to stories.

> I have sent the money to your bank account; however, you must withdraw it within sixteen days.

Apostrophes indicate either 1) letters that have been removed to form contractions (such has *have not = haven't*) or 2) possession (*the letter of Jack = Jack's letter*).

Be careful not to confuse words that sound the same but have a different meaning when spelled with an apostrophe. Remember, your spellchecker will not be able to find this kind of mistake!

your/you're
- Always check **your** writing.
- Find out the name of the person **you're** writing to. (= **you are**)

their/there/they're
- Please send the organization **their** money.
- I have never been **there**.
- I don't know where **they're** from. (= **they are**)

its/it's
- I can't remember **its** name.
- **It's** not polite to use lots of abbreviations in email. (= **it is**)

If you're having trouble deciding whether to use an apostrophe, stop and consider what you are trying to say. For example, if you want to say *you are*, then *you're* is the spelling, not *your*. Don't just guess, and don't just use one of each, like this:

> Here is what we needed from you to complete the transfer, You' re Name, Your Address ID CARD COPY and Your Telephone Number

Capitalization

Always capitalize the following:

- The first word used in a salutation:

    X dearest Beloved
    √ Dearest beloved

- Names and proper nouns (countries, languages, cities, and so on):

    X tanya
    √ Tanya

    X albania
    √ Albania

- The first person pronoun:

    X …and that is why i am writing…
    √ …and that is why I am writing…

- The first letter of the first word in a sentence:

    X there is a chance…
    √ There is a chance…

- The first word used in a closing:

    X   best Regards
    XX BEST REGARDS
    √   Best regards

There are a few additional rules for capitalization, but these are the basics and the ones you should be sure to follow. It should go without saying that a writer should not go around capitalizing words that don't need capitalizing, and certainly should never CAPITALIZE ALL THE LETTERS OF THE WORDS or even SOME of them LIKE THIS. It *should* go without saying, but based on the example below, we felt we should say it anyway:

Subject: The Internet Spy Guide! Find Out Info About Anyone!

HALLO! ARE YOU READY TO KNOW?!! CONFEDENTIAL: The SOFTWARE they want BANNED in all 50 STATES. WHY? Because these SECRETS were never intended to reach your eyes...Get FACTS on ANYONE using the INTERNENT!!! Locate Missing Persons, FIND Lost Relatives, obtain Adresses and Phone Numbers of old school friends, even Skip Trace Dead Beat Spouses. This is not a Private Investigator, but a sophisticated SOFTWARE program DESIGNED to automatically CRACK YOUR CASE with links to thousands of Public Record Databases.

Obviously, this writer thinks that writing the words he feels are important in capital letters is a good way of making sure the reader pays attention to those important words. Well, he's wrong. All those capital letters make us feel like we're being shouted at. This is never a nice feeling to have, but it's particularly annoying when a writer shouts out a spelling error like CONFEDENTIAL!!! and then makes that even worse by adding three unnecessary exclamation marks.

Please don't do this. Just capitalize the first letter of the words that need to be capitalized, and no more than that. If your letter is well written, the reader will understand what the important words are. If you feel you must draw a reader's attention to a word or phrase, use italics or bold, but remember that overusing them is annoying and unprofessional.

WALL OF SHAME

From: **Johan Cleff** <ritahawel@xxxxxxx.com>
Date: Sun, Feb 2, 2014 at 11:57 AM
Subject:
To:

Are you financially Squeezed? * Do you seek funds to pay off credits and debts * Do you seek finance to set up your own business? ONLY REPLY TO:accreditedlenders.xx.xxx@xxxxx.com

Unit 3 Exercises

Work alone. Correct the punctuation and capitalization mistakes in Tanya's letter and the letters that follow. Then compare your corrections with a partner, if possible. Check your answers at the back of the book.

1.

> dearest beloved,
>
> How are you? i hope, all is ok! My name, is tanya, from a small Village near tirana, albania I\'m a rather shy girl at first. i open up a little more, as i get to know someone. i attache my Foto. i hope you liked it. i am a not a clever girl but I am kind. I like, craftwork, baking, sewing and so on. i do many things to make myself HAPPY for example, playing piano, DANCING to music, doing aerobics and listening to STORIES. i am looking for a strong decent man. i do not know what to write because i never used the Internet for acquaintance before. Write to ME if you want to, learn more about me; And see my other pictures. i will, WAIT YOUR LETTER. Write to me soon, i will send another FOTO.
>
> take Care!
>
> tanya
>
> Ps: there is the chance, We can do the business, also.

2.

> If your bank, immediately closed your account, the funds will BOUNCE BACK TO US. When we receive the Funds, we will automatically, deposit them to the verified bank account, on file. Once this happens you will have THREE DAYS to contact us give us your information and tell us what to do with your funds.
>
> Kaw valley state bank

3.

> Subject: The Internet Spy Guide! Find Out Info About Anyone!
>
> HALLO! ARE YOU READY TO know?!! CONFEDENTIAL!!!: The SOFTWARE they want BANNED in all 50 STATES. WHY? Because these SECRETS were never intended to reach your eyes...Get FACTS on ANYONE using the INTERNENT!!! Locate Missing Persons, FIND Lost Relatives, obtain Adresses and Phone Numbers of old school friends, even Skip Trace Dead Beat Spouses. This is not a Private Investigator, but a sophisticated SOFTWARE program DESIGNED to automatically CRACK YOUR CASE with links to thousands of Public Record Databases.

4.

> HI
>
> My Name is trevor emmanuel,.

5.

> REMEMBER TO SEND THEM YOUR CURRENT FOLLOWINGS INFORMATION'S:
> YOUR FULL NAME ....
> YOUR HOME ADDRESS....
> YOU'RE CURRENT PHONE NUMBERS..... HOME
> YOU'RE CELL NUMBERS.....
> YOU PERSONAL IDENTIFICATION.....

SPELLING

It is extremely important for every word in a business letter to be spelled correctly. Business email is not a text message or an online forum post to your friends; it's *business*. Misspelled words are unprofessional. If recipients of your emails find words that are misspelled – even if they're typing mistakes – their opinion of you and your company will be negatively affected.

Spellcheckers

Many email programs have spellcheckers included. If yours doesn't, then write your email first in a word processing program that has a spellchecker. Then, of course, you must actually *use* the spellchecker.

Remember, though, that a spellchecker cannot catch every mistake, even though it will catch many.

A spellchecker can catch words that are not correct English at all. For example, look at this paragraph:

> Actually I am new to this place and am looking for a gud friend , whom I can hang out with but it gonna be with some gud people, my friend she gave me your email id .you gottaa join me now and come online

A spellchecker will let you know that *gud* and *gonna* and *gottaa* are not spelled correctly. You will have to know, of course, that the correct spellings are *good* and *going to* and *have got to*, or know somebody who can help you.

A spellcheck program can also find simple typos – typing errors – like this one:

> You are not expected to pay for the tansfer charge as that will be deducted from the funds once the remittance is done.

Probably the person typing meant to write *transfer*, but missed the letter *r*.

However, a spellchecker cannot find words that exist in English words, but are not used correctly. For example, look at the word *gravy* in the excerpt below (sorry about all the capital letters; this scammer had not yet read Unit 3):

> THIS IS BECAUSE THE CANCER STAGE HAS GOTTEN TO A VERY GRAVY STAGE SO I BEG FOR YOUR HELP BEFORE I REACH THE STAGE OF COMATOSE.

Gravy is a word in English; however, it means a kind of sauce made from the fat and juices of cooked meat. The writer should have used the word *grave* here, meaning "serious." But because *gravy* is a real word, a spellchecker cannot point out the mistake.

In fact, sometimes spellcheckers can make this kind of mistake for you. For example, if the writer mistypes *grave* by typing just "grav," the spellchecker might suggest *gravy*, and a writer who isn't being careful enough would accept the suggestion. The autocorrect function of smartphones often creates this type of error. In fact, there is a website devoted to funny smartphone errors of this type.

It is difficult to catch this kind of mistake. You have to read and reread your email several times to be sure you are using the words you want. Reading your email out loud is a very useful way to help you catch mistakes.

It's also important not to use words if you don't know what they mean, because you will not be able to tell if you are using them correctly. Even if you see a word used somewhere else (especially online), if you do not know what the word means, you cannot tell if someone else is using it correctly or not.

For example, there is an expression used in English used to about especially serious illnesses: *to defy treatment*. This means that the illness or disease was stronger than the medicine or procedure used against it. The past tense of *defy* is *defied*. However, there is a similarly spelled word in English, *defile*, that means to spoil something or make it dirty. Apparently, a scammer somewhere confused the two words. Because other scammers then copied the first scammer's email, you now see that phrase turn up in letters from different people. Here is a recent collection from my spam folder. Notice the similarities!

My name is Mr. Mikhael Geha, Nationality Lebanese I based in Thailand, I have diagnosed with Esophageal Cancer that was discovered very late due to my laxity in caring for my health. It has defiled all form of medicine and right now, I have only about a few months to live according to medical experts.

I am HASSAN IBRAHIM a merchant in DUBAI, I have been diagnosed with esophageal cancer, it has defiled all forms of medical treatment, and right now I have only about a few months to live, according to medical experts

My name is Mrs. Rosemary Nelson from California I have been diagnosed with Esophageal cancer. It has defiled all forms of medical treatment, and right now I have only about a few months to live, according to medical experts.

I am tiago josebrasco ., A Hong Kong national bases in England, I was browsing and I saw your e-mail So i decided to write you if your e-mail is real, I have been diagnosed with esophageal cancer. It has defiled all forms of medical treatment, and right now I have only about a few months to live.

I am Calvolta iyon ferry., A Hong Kong national bases in England, I was browsing and I saw your e-mail as donor to Church, Roads, school Scholarship, So i decided to write you if your e-mail is real, I have been diagnosed with esophageal cancer. It has defiled all forms of medical treatment, and right now I have only about a few months to live.

Finally, be careful with commonly confused homonyms (words that sound the same, but are spelled differently) as well as words that are spelled similarly. Here are a few of these, with example sentences of typical meanings.

accept / except
• Do not **accept** packages from strangers – especially if you have to pay to receive them. (*accept* = verb)
• I attended every class **except** one in November, when I was sick. (*except* = preposition)

advice / advise
• I would like your **advice**. (*advice* = noun)
• Please **advise** me about what to do. (*advise* = verb)

loose / lose
• The handle on this door is **loose**. It might come off. (*loose* = adjective)
• Don't be unhappy if you **lose**. It's only a game. (*lose* = verb)

message / massage
• May I leave a **message** for Mr. King? (*message* = noun)
• If you have tension in your neck and shoulders, you might benefit from a professional **massage**. (*massage* = also a noun, but one with a very different meaning from message)

past / passed
• She ran **past** my house. (*past* = preposition)
• I **passed** her on my way to school. (*passed* = verb)

then / than
• First I ate lunch, and **then** I went back to work. (*then* = adverb)
• You are a better writer **than** I am. (*than* = subordinating conjunction. Use it with comparisons.)

Of course, there are many more commonly confused words in English. This book can't list them all, or you'd never get to the other chapters. Remember that a good dictionary is your friend. Also, if you have a friend who is a proficient speaker of English, you can ask that person to check your email after you write it. After all, you have nothing to hide. (Do you?)

Unit 4 Exercises

Work alone. Find all of the misspelled words in the examples below. There could be one or more than one mistake in each example. Then, if you are working in a class, compare your answers with a partner (you can also discuss any other mistakes you find). If you are working alone, check your answers in the back of the book.

By the way – it is not cheating to use a dictionary!

1.

> Just like I stated in my first email, this paymen includes every foreign contractors that may have not received their contract sum, and people that have had an unfinished transaction or international businesses that failed due to Government problems etc.

2.

> MY NAME IS MRS LINDA BRUNO, I'M SUFFERING FROM TROAT CANCER.

3.

> I would have paid that but they said no because they
>
> don't know when you will contact them and in the case of
>
> demurrage. You have to contact CITY LINK Couriers Limited
>
> now for the delivery of your Draft with this information
>
> bellow;

4.

> I wish to introduce to you a profitable deal worth over Fourty eight million US dollars, I need your permission before I provide details

5.

> Believe me but I told you before that I cannot deceive you because my Bible says what shall it profit a man to gain material things and
> Loose your soul, any way their is good news now, i raised some money To help you out and make sure that your payment will be release to you The same day you send the $95 as well.

6.

> I was lead by the Almighty to send this mail to you after serious thought of all emails I saw on the internet. Please treat this seriously. I have all documents of deposit of this fund to proove I hope to hear from you soonest before I go.

7.

> We provide a concept that will allow anyone with sufficient work experience to obtain a fully verifiable Unievrsity Dgeree. Doctoarte, Bcahelors or Docotrate. Within a few weeks, you can become a college graduate!

8.

> We guarantee you 100% safety and wish you the best of luck. And NOTE: If you are been contact by anyone to send anymore fee kindly forward it to MR JOHN WILL and stop anyfurther cummication with those fraudstar for your own safety.

GRAMMAR

Grammatical mistakes seriously discredit your business letter. They can make you look ignorant, unintelligent, careless – or all three. If English is not your first language, these conclusions might not be true. However, that doesn't stop people from drawing them. Therefore, you want to take great care to make your email as correct as possible.

Improving your grammar

What can you do if your English is not proficient?

It is not possible in this book to teach you all of the English grammar rules you will need. If you have weaknesses, we suggest taking an English class or using self-study materials to improve your grammar. Of course, if you need to send an email tomorrow morning, you can't perfect your grammar tonight. It takes some time. Study and practice a little each day, and you will improve over time.

Here are some self-study resources that we recommend to both native and non-native speakers of English who need to brush up on or improve their English grammar and usage:

Websites: (These are free to use)
• The Online Writing Lab (OWL) at Purdue University:
https://owl.english.purdue.edu/
• The Guide to Grammar and Writing, sponsored by the Capital Community College Foundation:
http://grammar.ccc.commnet.edu/grammar/
• The Internet Grammar of English course (British English):
http://www.ucl.ac.uk/internet-grammar/

Textbooks: (These must be purchased or borrowed from a library)
• *English Grammar in Use*, by Raymond Murphy (Cambridge University Press) (three levels)
• *Understanding English Grammar*, by Betty Azar (Pearson Education) (three levels)
• *Oxford Practice Grammar*, various authors (Oxford University Press)

In the meantime, use these hints to improve your emails:

1) Write short sentences. Short, manageable sentences are more likely to be clear and correct. It is better to write three short correct sentences than one long incorrect one.

2) Use expressions and patterns that you know well. This is not the time to experiment with grammar you are only half sure of. This isn't creative writing or poetry. This is business. Your primary concern isn't to sound fancy, but to convey information accurately and efficiently.

3) Have your email checked by someone proficient in English before you send it. Even native speakers get others to check important documents for them. In fact, we had seven English teachers, university professors, and authors check this textbook before we published it.

Common errors

Here are some common types of grammatical mistakes we noticed in letters we have received. The first sentence (quoted exactly as we received it) is incorrect, indicated by an X; the correct version is marked below with a √ mark. The target structures are underlined.

- **Subject-verb agreement**:

    X Since his death <u>nobody have show up</u> to claim the deposit.
    √ Since his death, <u>nobody has shown up</u> to claim the deposit.

    X I came across your <u>profile</u> which really <u>sound</u> so interesting of you.
    √ I came across your <u>profile</u>, which really <u>sounds</u> very interesting.

- **Singular/plural issues** (including problems with **count** and **noncount nouns**):

    X He is going to work with the legal chamber and Bank to secure <u>this funds</u> in a very proper and legal manner and he will make all <u>arrangement</u> in your name…
    √ He is going to work with the legal chamber and the bank to secure <u>these funds</u> in a very proper and legal manner, and he will make all <u>arrangements</u> in your name…

X Note that you have to contact my private email for more <u>informations</u>
√ Note that you have to contact my private email for more <u>information</u>.

X We give out <u>loan</u> ranging from $5, 000.00 to <u>maximum</u> $5,000, 000.00 to individuals in need of financial assistance
√ We give out <u>loans</u> ranging from $5,000.00 to <u>a maximum of</u> $5,000, 000.00 to individuals in need of financial assistance.

- **Infinitives vs. gerunds:**

  X It may surprise you <u>receiving</u> this mail from me, since there was no previous correspondence between us.
  √ It may surprise you <u>to receive</u> this mail from me, since there was no previous correspondence between us.

  X BY TOMORROW, YOU WILL START <u>TO BE RECEIVING</u> YOUR FIRST $5000 US DOLLARS DAILY
  √ By tomorrow, you will start <u>to receive</u> the first of your daily $5000 payments.

- **Modals:**

  X i will like to know more about you
  √ I would like to know more about you.

  X Hello gorgeous! If you were a burger in Mc'Donald, i'<u>ll</u> call you Mc'gorgeous.
  √ Hello, gorgeous! If you were a burger at McDonald's, I'<u>d</u> …

You know what? Do not compare a woman to a burger at McDonald's. With any kind of grammar.

- **Verb tense and aspect:**

  X You <u>shall be earn</u> a monthly wage of $3000 USD if you are able to complete every assignment you are given without any delay.
  √ You <u>will earn</u> a monthly wage of $3000 USD if you are able to complete every assignment you are given without delay.

  X We issued the ATM card because we <u>find</u> out that it was the best way to get your funds <u>delivering</u> to you…
  √ We issued the ATM card because we <u>found</u> out that it was the best way to get your funds <u>delivered</u> to you…

- **Prepositions:**

    X i must confess you look beautiful <u>on</u> your pictures
    √ I must confess you look beautiful <u>in</u> your pictures.

    X Have you been <u>denied of a loan</u> from your bank or any financial firm?
    √ Have you been <u>denied a loan</u> from your bank or any financial firm?

- **Word forms:**

    X What you have to do now is to contact the FedEx Courier Service as soon as possible to know when they will deliver your package to you because of the <u>expiring</u> date.
    √ What you have to do now is to contact the FedEx courier service as soon as possible to know when they will deliver your package because of the <u>expiration</u> date.

    X Getting a legitimate loan has always been a huge problem to clients who have <u>financially in needs</u>.
    √ Getting a legitimate loan has always been a huge problem for clients who have <u>financial needs</u>.

- **Pronouns:**

    X Your email address was submitted to my wife and <u>I</u> by the Google Management Team.
    √ Your email address was submitted to my wife and <u>me</u> by the Google Management Team.

    X Do to our ongoing account protection all customers are advised to review <u>your</u> online access,
    √ Due to our ongoing account protection, all customers are advised to review <u>their</u> online access.

Choose the letter of the correct sentence. Then check your answers at the back of the book.

1.

    a. Like I stated earlier, the crediting re-activation, delivery and the company registration charges has been paid by me…

    b. As I stated earlier, the crediting re-activation, delivery, and the company registration charges have been paid by me…

2.

    a. Note that your package was registered as a box of African cloth.

    b. Note: your package was register as box of Africa cloth.

3.

    a. Your fund will now be packed in a box and taken to the diplomatic courier service for immediate shipment.

    b. Your fund will now package in box and take to the diplomatic courier service for immediate shipment.

4.

    a. I advice that you urgently respond to this message.

    b. I advise you to urgently respond to this message.

5.

    a. I HAVE TO HIRE A LAWYER BEFORE THAT CAN BE DONE SINCE YOU THE BENEFICIARY OF THE CHEQUE IS NOT HERE.

    b. I have to hire a lawyer before that can be done since you, the beneficiary of the cheque, are not here.

Work with a partner or alone. Find and correct the mistakes in the following excerpts.

6. (at least three mistakes, not counting the capital letters, which you may also correct)

> For your information, I have paid for the delivering Charge, Insurance premium and Clearance Certificate Fees of the Cheque showing that it is not a Drug Money or meant to sponsor Terrorist attack in your Country.

7. (three mistakes)

> Remember, I supposed to have traveled last week but the weather is too bad. I will be leaving to Paraguay tomorrow.

WALL OF SHAME

From: Shilpi@Intel <notification@xxxxxx.net>
Date: Wed, Feb 26, 2014 at 2:48 AM
Subject: Hi , view my pic attached

Hi ,
Just wanted you to know that yesterday I joined Socialmoto, **World's biggest Career Networking site**. Actually I am new to this place and am looking for a gud friend , whom I can hang out with but it gonna be with some gud people during holidays , my friend she gave me your email id .you gottaa join me now and come online , nowadays we can chat as i have lots of spare time , kidding hehe :)

My album: Visit this to see my pics
http://www.xxxxxxxxxxxxxxxxxxxxxxxxxxxxxxxxxxxxx

My profile:
http://www.xxxxxxxxxxxxxxxxxxxxxxxxxxxxxxxxxxxxx

To join simply come here.
http://www.xxxxxxxxxxxxxxxxxxxxxxxxxxxxxxxxxxxxx

When you come here ping me, i will be online if by any sense i am not there.

Thanks,
Shilpi
Developer@Intel

I have attached my details.
Shilpi

COMMON EXPRESSIONS

Business letters are not creative writing. This is not the time to look for new and unusual ways to express your thoughts. You want to communicate efficiently and accurately. For this reason, business letters contain many standard phrases that everyone recognizes. Using these standard phrases shows your recipient that you know what you're doing; that you belong to the community of successful business people.

Recognizing inappropriate language

What would your reaction be if you received the following email in your inbox?

[subject line: HELLO DEAR]

I am Mr Newton Dennis from a bank.I need you to keep this confidential,Late president Muammar Gaddafi of (Libya) has a secret account worth $20.5 Million United state dollars.i will be entitled to 50% you will get 50% for your assistance , if you are willing to receive this money.contact me through this email (newtondennis12@xxxxxx.com)

Like most people, you would probably either never finish reading it, or laugh out loud as you read it through. If you read the whole thing, you might then want to share it with a friend or two (even though Mr. Newton Dennis has asked for confidentiality) so they could laugh, too. Then, you'd delete it from your inbox and hope to never hear from Mr. Dennis again. This certainly is not what the writer hopes that you'll do, but since he's broken almost all the rules for good business writing, what can he expect, really?

He probably never expected his letter would wind up in a book like this, but since it did, and because we are in the business of writing good business letters, let's take a closer look at Mr. Newton Dennis's letter.

Given what you already know, how many things can you find wrong with it? Take a moment and think about this before reading on.

Yes, that's right. Mr. Dennis has used an inappropriate subject heading, failed to run a spellcheck, does not indicate that he knows who he is writing this letter to, never mentions which bank he works for (just "a bank"? Really?), makes several punctuation and grammar errors, and yet would like us to believe that somehow he's found Muammar Gaddafi's secret bank account and knows how much is in it: $20.5 million dollars.

He also fails to use any of the standard phrases and sentences that very often appear in business letters. Doing so probably would not make us believe he really knows where this secret bank account is or that we could get 10.25 million dollars by contacting Mr. Dennis; but at least he'd have a better letter.

Standard parts of a letter

1. Introduction and Notification

It's a little weird for Mr. Dennis to begin his letter by identifying himself, and it wouldn't be any less weird if he'd mentioned the name of the bank where he works and his position there. Such information belongs at the end of the letter, following the signature, not at the beginning (see Unit 2). Mr. Dennis's letter could be made better by simply getting to the point and starting off with something like this:

Dear Mr. Sandy,

I am writing to let you know that I am in possession of some confidential information regarding Muammar Gaddafi's secret bank account in Libya.

Not only does the writer gain my confidence by greeting me by name, but he also uses *I am writing to let you know that* to begin his letter. Other phrases he could have used include:

- I am writing to tell you about…
- I am happy to inform you that…
- It is my pleasure to tell you that…
- I am contacting you because…

2. Going into Detail

Rather than an abrupt request to keep his forthcoming message a secret, Mr. Dennis could have just skipped all that and provided additional details, starting with a sentence like one of these:

- Allow me to explain.
- Let me tell you more.
- Here are some of the specific points.

> I am writing to let you know that I am in possession of some confidential information regarding Muammar Gaddafi's secret bank account in Libya. **Allow me to explain.**

And this of course is where Mr. Dennis would provide a brief outline of how he got this information, why this information might be important for me or my company, and what action he would like me to take.

3. Asking for Assistance

Next, one of these phrases would help Mr. Dennis as he makes his request for my assistance in this matter.

- I would be grateful if you would / could …
- It would be helpful if you would / could…
- I would like to ask you to please…

> I am writing to let you know that I am in possession of some confidential information regarding Muammar Gaddafi's secret bank account in Libya. Allow me to explain. [explanation] **I would be grateful if you would** please provide me with your contact information by emailing me directly at newtondennis12@xxxxxx.com.

4. Offering Assistance

Given the nature of the request, it's probably safe to assume that the reader would want some more information. Mr. Dennis could have used one of these phrases to offer some:

- I would be happy to…
- If I can be of further assistance, please contact me at…
- If you have any questions, please do not hesitate to contact me by…

I am writing to let you know that I am in possession of some confidential information regarding Muammar Gaddafi's secret bank account in Libya. Allow me to explain. [explanation] I would be grateful if you would please provide me with your contact information by emailing me directly at newtondennis12@xxxxxx.com. **I would be happy to** provide you with further information or to answer any questions you might have.

5. Enclosing / Attaching Documents

Although it's unlikely that many people would feel safe opening an attachment from Mr. Dennis, he could inspire more confidence by providing detailed information about his proposal in a separate document attached to a brief email. When doing this, a writer might use a phrase like one of these:

- Please find [my resume] attached.
- For your reference, I am attaching [a business report] as a .pdf.
- To help you understand the process more clearly, I am attaching [a diagram] as a Word document.

I am writing to let you know that I am in possession of some confidential information regarding Muammar Gaddafi's secret bank account in Libya. Allow me to explain. [explanation]

I would be grateful if you would please provide me with your contact information by emailing me directly at newtondennis12@xxxxxx.com. I would be happy to provide you with further information or to answer any questions you might have.

For your reference, I am attaching a file containing detailed information about the account and an outline of the procedures we will need to follow in order to transfer the funds.

(Note, however, that many people will not click on a link or open an attachment from somebody they do not already know. You will be more likely to send attachments in subsequent messages after you have established trust.)

6. Requesting a Reply

Obviously, Mr. Dennis wants a reply to his letter, so he could use one or more of these sentences to let the reader politely know this.

- I'm looking forward to hearing from you.
- I would appreciate your prompt reply.

I am writing to let you know that I am in possession of some confidential information regarding Muammar Gaddafi's secret bank account in Libya. Allow me to explain. [explanation]
I would be grateful if you would please provide me with your contact information by emailing me directly at newtondennis12@xxxxxx.com. I would be happy to provide you with further information or to answer any questions you might have.

For your reference, I am attaching a file containing detailed information about the account and an outline of the procedures we will need to follow in order to transfer the funds.

I look forward to hearing back from you. I would appreciate receiving a prompt reply.

7. Closing the Letter

Given that this is a business letter, the proper sign off would be something like

Sincerely,

To be even more polite, Mr. Dennis could use

Yours sincerely,

He could even use

Yours truly,

Following the closing, Mr. Dennis should give his full name, his place of employment, and his position there, so that his entire letter might look like this:

Dear Mr. Sandy,

I am writing to let you know that I am in possession of some confidential information regarding Muammar Gaddafi's secret bank account in Libya. Allow me to explain. [Explanantion].

I would be grateful if you would please provide me with your contact information by emailing me directly at newtondennis12@xxxxxx.com. I would be happy to provide you with further information or to answer any questions you might have.

For your reference, I am attaching a file containing detailed information about the account and an outline of the procedures we will need to follow in order to transfer the funds.

I look forward to hearing back from you. I would appreciate receiving a prompt reply.

Sincerely,

Newton Dennis
Branch Manager
United Bank of Nairobi

It would help further if Mr. Dennis had provided an email address that indicated that he actually works at this bank, rather than emailing from a hotmail account.

WALL OF SHAME

From: Rifaat Al <assadal@xxxxxx.rthk.hk>
Date: Mon, Feb 3, 2014 at 3:45 PM
Subject: Hi
To:

I understand you will be shocked at my email,I am a Syrian citizen, I use to be a member of the Regime in Syria but i ran out of my country because of the civil war,i feel i might die any time soon my nephew the president want to kill us all if we do not support his government. I am contacting you because of my children, i need you to help me keep my funds and also invest for my children, the people I have trusted failed me so badly. i do not know how long i can hang on. Please get back to me let me give you details of my self and how the funds will be transferred to you for a safe keep for the children.Please email me now. EMAIL;
assadrifaat65@xxxxxx.com.hk

1. What are some other ways Mr. Dennis could make his letter more businesslike and more believable? Discuss your ideas with a partner, or just reflect silently. Imagine that you are the receiver of this letter from Mr. Dennis. What would make it more believable and persuasive to you?

2. Work alone. Do your best to correct the errors in this letter. Then, use some of the phrases introduced in this unit to write a more appropriate, more businesslike letter. Address your letter to a specific person. If you cannot think of anyone you'd like to write to, you may address your letter to one of the authors of this book.

Attention Beneficiary,

I am Mr. Oosthuizen of IMF Head Office in Washington DC. Your email appeared among the beneficiaries, who will receive a part-payment of your contractual sum of $8.5 Million US Dollars and has been approved already for months. You are requested to get back to me for more direction and instruction on how to receive your fund. However, we received an email from one Mrs. Virgie Brown who told us that she is your next of kin and that you died in a car accident last week. She has also submitted her account for us to transfer the fund to her. We want to hear from you before we can make the transfer to confirm if you are dead or not. Please in confirmation that you are still alive, you are advised to reconfirm the below listed information to enable us facilitate an immediate payment for you.

1 Your full names
2 Your present contact address.
3 Your telephone & Fax numbers.
4 Your Occupations/age/sex.
5 Your Private Email Address.

Once again, I apologize to you on behalf of IMF (International Monetary Fund) for failure to pay your funds in time, which according to records in the system had been long overdue.

From: Ray Ugo <office5077@xxxxxx.net>
Date: Thu, Feb 6, 2014 at 12:52 PM
Subject: HELLO
To: office5077@xxxxxx.net

Dear Friend,
I have been waiting for you since to come down here and pick your consignment but i did not heard anything from you since then, I have deposited the US$5,000,000.00 with the ALINCO SECURITY COMPANY here in Nigeria, because I traveled to Japan to see my boss and I will not come back till next year ending. I have arranged with the ALINCO SECURITY COMPANY to get your US$5,000,000.00 to you this month and they will be coming to you with the fund inside black portfolio, I would have deposited the fund with Bank for transfer into your own account but the procedure of Bank is too much and they will required enough fee.

I drop your delivery details with the ALINCO SECURITY COMPANY but I will like you to re-confirm the information to them again so that they will not be any mistake when coming with the fund. Send the below information to the ALINCO SECURITY COMPANY.

(1)Full name:

(2)Address:

(3)Tel:

I want you to know that you have all right to declare how you want to receive your fund, I would have prefer the fund to be transfer to you but I make some searches about the Bank transfer and they told me that it will cost you the sum of US$1500 to transfer the US$5,000,000.00 into your account. But I have deposited the US$5,000,000.00 in cash to the ALINCO SECURITY COMPANY, below is the ALINCO SECURITY COMPANY contact.

Director: Mr. Paul Ego.
Mobile: +555-809-6991-748
Email: (alinco011@xxxxxx.com)

I have paid the delivery charges and insurance fee to the ALINCO SECURITY COMPANY.
The only Money that the ALINCO SECURITY COMPANY will require from you is $75 Dollars for demurrage, if you can pay the $75 Dollars to them, they will proceed and get the US$5,000,000.00 to you in your Country.Pls if you want to contact the ALINCO SECURITY COMPANY, you are to contact them with your portfolio code number which is (PPL111RSS) and your address where you want them to deliver the cash to.You are to pay the $75 to the ALINCO SECURITY COMPANY to enable them to proceed and get the cash to you,don't fail to resend your information to them for your own good.

Regards,
Mr.Ray Ugo

APPROPRIATE TOPICS

There is one appropriate topic for your business letter, and that is – we do hope this won't come as a surprise – business. Topics that may be perfectly normal in a friendly personal letter, such as the weather, your family, your reader's family, your health, your political views, or your religious views, do not belong in a business letter. To some extent, this is cultural. There are other cultures in which some of these topics may be referred to even in business letters. However, if you are writing in English, avoid these topics or your reader may not trust you enough to conduct business.

Recognizing inappropriate topics

Let's analyze the topic mistakes this writer, a Mrs. Jane Milne Robert, is making.

> Dear,
>
> Good day to you and your family today.

Right away, the email starts badly. Mrs. Robert is probably trying to be friendly, but she misses her first chance by not including my name. Then before the first sentence is finished, she has veered off to an irrelevant topic. Why is she writing to my family? If she doesn't know my name, how could she know anything about my family?

I am sure this mail would be coming to you as a surprise since we have never met before and you would also be asking why I have decided to chose you amongst the numerous internet users in the world, precisely I cannot say why I have chosen you but do not be worried for I come in peace and something very positive is about to happen to your life right now and to the lives of others through you if only you can carefully read and digest the message below. The internet has made the world a global village where you can reach anybody you have not met before.

Well, she is right about the surprise. But it's weak to tell someone that you cannot say why you are writing. The whole purpose of the first paragraph of a business email is to explain why you *are* writing – and why you are writing specifically to me.

And why is she telling me about a global village? This is an email. It should be short and direct, not sum up the last 50 or 100 years of human civilization.

Before I move further, permit me to give you a little of my biography, I am Mother Jane milne Robert, 87 Years old woman and the wife of Late Sir Milne Robert who died in a Plane crash on Monday the 7th of September 1998 GMT 14:22 UK while they were flying from New York to Geneva.

No, no, no. I do not want a little of your biography. I don't care about your age or the name of your husband. I don't need to know how he died, where he was flying, or the time of his death – down to the time zone and the minute. It's all irrelevant information.

Please see site below for more information.
http://www.cnn.com/WORLD/9809/swissair.victims.list/index.html

No.

Because of the easy spread of Internet viruses, people who don't know you won't want to click on any links.

After the death of my husband I became the Head of his investment and now that I am old and weak I have decided to spend the rest of my life with my family and loved ones whom I never had time for during the course of my business life, but before the death of my husband we had a plan to use the last days of our lives to donate half of what we have worked for to the less privilege and charity homes and the other half for ourselves, family members and close friends, and it is so unfortunate that my husband is not alive today to do this with me and I am very weak and old now, hence I have decided to do this philanthropic work on behalf of my late husband and I.

Wow. Tear down your wall of text! What is the message here? What does the writer want? I have no idea, because even after 138 words, she has not said what she wants. Surely it's coming soon, though…

Presently, I have willed out almost half of our assets to several charity homes and to some of the less privilege in different countries.
Despite the agreement between my late husband and I to give aid to the deprived, we also agreed to render support to an individual we have not meet before in life due to the fact when we were still young in life we receive an anonymous help from an individual we did not know and which we have not being able to know or met again till date, the impact we got from such gestsure made us want to do same.

Nope. I still have no idea what she wants. I don't know anything more about her except that her spellchecker is not working or that she is too lazy to use it. There is no such thing as a "gestsure."

I am sorry to inform you that you will never have the chance to know me because I have just concluded the assignment which my husband and I have agreed upon before his sudden death and you happened to be the beneficiary of our last WILL, irrespective of your previous financial status, hence I need you to do me a favor by accepting our offer that will cost you nothing.

Don't be sorry; I'm not. But even though we're coming closer to what must be the purpose of the letter – there is some sort of offer – I still have no idea what the letter is about.

And you know what? I don't even care anymore. I'm not even going to finish reading.

There seems to be some belief (or perhaps hope) that someone will do business with you if you are sick; and that if you are close to death, they'll be doubly likely to trust you.

This is not true.

Upon reading that you have cancer, a new business contact does not think, "Wow, I should send you money." No, the thought is, "Are you insane? What are you doing on the Internet? Go to a doctor!" Business is not built on pity. The people who care for you when your health is bad will be your family, your friends, or paid caregivers – not strangers you are asking for money or favors. Furthermore, most people prefer to begin business relationships that will last for some time. For that reason, they may not be so keen to enter into negotiations with someone who assures them they will be dead soon:

I am Mrs. Rosemarie Blumen Moldenhauer born in Munich, Germany with e-mail address: (rosemarieblumenm2@xxxxxx.com), my husband worked with gold exploration company in India/Asia for 29 years. Before his death in February 2011 in Christchurch earthquake in New Zealand, He deposited the sum of £ 10,000,000.00 GBP with a Bank in London/United Kingdom, The Fund Was Meant To Open a charitable home for the less privilege and named me his wife as the beneficiary of this trust fund as the beneficiary of the funds but due to my present ill health I prefer to rather issue a letter of authorization to somebody to receive it on my behalf as I cannot come over due to my health condition. So I prefer to rather issue a letter of authorization to somebody to receive it on my behalf as I cannot come over due to my health condition

I'm in a hospital in India/Asia now where I have been undergoing treatment for esophageal cancer. I have since lost my ability to talk, and my doctors have told me that I have only a few weeks to live. My husband's family want me dead to acquire this wealth. I cannot live with the agony of entrusting this huge responsibility to any of them as they are unbelievers.

Oh, no. Not esophageal cancer again, the scourge of the Internet! And let me guess – it has defiled all medical treatment.

The last line of that paragraph brings us to another topic to avoid: religion. If you don't know the religious faith of the person you're writing to, don't mention your own. In fact, even if you *do* know your recipient's religious faith, and it happens to be the same as your own, it would be very unusual to bring it up in an English-language business letter unless your business was specifically about religion (such as building a church). Mentioning religion doesn't make you seem more honest or trustworthy; it makes you seem as if you have no idea how to conduct business appropriately.

Occasionally in English-language business letters, you will see some non-business references. Someone might say, "Have a nice weekend" or even "Hope you're enjoying the hot weather." However, references like these are not made until the two people emailing have established some kind of relationship or connection. You should not use them in a first contact business letter to a stranger.

WALL OF SHAME

From: GEN.GENE LEON <imf0088@xxxxxxx.com.tw>
Date: Fri, Jan 31, 2014 at 11:57 AM
Subject: YOUR EMAIL IS IMPORTANT TO US!! REPLY..
To:

I.M.F WORLD REGULATORY OFFICE
International Monetary Fund,
0088 Circle Abuja Nigeria.
SWIFT: IMFDUS3WXXX
Telephone Operator: +234-806-555-3305
Business Hours: Monday - Monday: 8:30 a.m. to 6:00 p.m

Greeting's
We are writhing to know if it's true that you are DEAD? Because we received a notification from one MR. GERSHON SHAPIRO of USA stating that you are DEAD and that you have giving him the right to claim your funds.He stated you died in a CAR accident. He has been calling us regarding this issue, but we cannot proceed with him until we confirm this within after 7 days of no respond.

Be advised that we have made all arrangements for you to receive and confirm your funds without any more stress, and without any further delay.

All we need to confirm now is you been DEAD Or still Alive. Because this MAN'S message brought shock to our minds. And we just can't proceed with him until we confirm if this is a reality OR not But if it happened we did not hear from you after 7 days, then we say: MAY YOUR SOUL REST IN PERFECT PEACE"

YOUR JOY AND SUCCESS REMAINS OUR GOAL.

May the peace of the Lord be with you wherever you may be now
Your Faithfully,
Mr.Gene Leon
Email:imf0088@xxxxxx.com

Unit 7 Exercises

There may be more than one for each exercise.

1. Which of the following topics are NOT appropriate in a business letter? Circle all of the correct answers.

    a. Your cancer
    b. Your esophagus
    c. Your esophageal cancer
    d. Your husband's death
    e. Your death
    f. Your unscrupulous family
    g. Your recipient's family
    h. Jesus
    i. Buddha
    j. Reasons you are poor now
    k. A marriage proposal
    l. Reference to any recent natural disaster such as a tsunami or earthquake
    m. Business

2. Work with a partner. Discuss everything in the two emails on the next pages that is not appropriate for a business letter. (If you are working alone, identify the inappropriate topics for yourself.) You may also discuss any other mistakes you see, using information from Units 1-6.

Letter A.

Dear friend,

My name is Allen Gomez. I got your profile from the (Email Directory) of your country

After going through your profile i deem it necessary to contact you for a business investment .I have great interest to invest in your country. I was once a U.S. Army deployed in Afghanistan. I got out of the Army because we made some million of US money worth $ 8,000,000.00 (Eight Million United States Dollars). We find this money in Afghanistan and managed to transfer the funds to London.

Unfortunately,three of my colleagues, involved in this operation died in Afghanistan and I was the only person left. Currently the fund is safe in a security company and finance in London.I later dropped out of the war because of my heart problem and my inability to hear properly. This is because my ears were hit by anti-aircraft shells.

I wanted to invest this money in your country, but have no body to trust, until I saw your profile and decided to write you. My purpose of contacting you is assist me to receive and invest this money $8,000,000,00USD in a project that will create jobs for the poor and less privileged. I will give 30% of the funds for your services. Get back to me if you can handle this project properly. Then lets agree.. I'm currently in the hospital with my laptop and I do not know if I can survive this condition.

Meanwhile, I'm in touch with a competent Lawyer who will clear the funds from the security company here in London and transfer the money to you in you.

Please keep this top secret from your friends and relations. I await your response for more details.

Yours sincerely
Allen Gomez.

Letter B. (Note: The original letter was all in bold, and also in a strange brown color, which we've changed to the standard business black.)

My Dear ,

I am writing this mail to you with tears and sorrow from my heart. With due respect ,trust and humanity, i appeal to you to exercise a little patience and read through my letter, I wish to contact you personally for a long term business relationship and investment assistance in your Country so i feel quite safe dealing with you in this important business having gone through your remarkable profile, honestly i am writing this email to you with pains, tears and sorrow from my heart, i will really like to have a good relationship with you and i have a special reason why i decided to contact you, i decided to contact you due to the urgency of my situation, My name is Precious Kipkalya Kones, 24yrs old female and I held from Kenya in East Africa. My father was the former Kenyan road Minister. He and Assistant Minister of Home Affairs Lorna Laboso had been on board the Cessna 210, which was headed to Kericho and crashed in a remote area called Kajong'a, in western Kenya. The plane crashed on the Tuesday 10th, June, 2008. You can read more about the crash through the below site:

http://edition.cnn.com/2008/WORLD/africa/06/10/kenya.crash/index.html

After the burial of my father, my stepmother and uncle conspired and sold my father's property to an Italian Expert rate which the shared the money among themselves and live nothing for me. I am constrained to contact you because of the abuse I am receiving from my wicked stepmother and uncle. They planned to take away all my late father's treasury and properties from me since the unexpected death of my beloved Father. Meanwhile i wanted to escape to the USA but they hide away my international passport and other valuable travelling documents. Luckily they did not discover where i kept my fathers File which contains important documents. So I decided to run to the refugee camp where i am presently seeking asylum under the United Nations High Commission for the Refugee here in Ouagadougou, Republic of Burkina Faso.

One faithful morning, I opened my father's briefcase and found out the documents which he has deposited huge amount of money in bank in

Burkina Faso with my name as the next of kin. I travelled to Burkina Faso to withdraw the money for a better life so that I can take care of myself and start a new life, on my arrival, the Bank Director whom I met in person told me that my father's instruction/will to the bank is that the money would only be release to me when I am married or present a trustee who will help me and invest the money overseas. I am in search of an honest and reliable person who will help me and stand as my trustee so that I will present him to the Bank for transfer of the money to his bank account overseas. I have chosen to contact you after my prayers and I believe that you will not betray my trust. But rather take me as your own sister.

Although, you may wonder why I am so soon revealing myself to you without knowing you, well I will say that my mind convince Ed me that you may be the true person to help me. More so, my father of blessed memory deposited the sum of (US$11.500, 000) Dollars in Bank with my name as the next of kin. However, I shall forward you with the necessary documents on confirmation of your acceptance to assist me for the transfer and statement of the fund in your country. As you will help me in an investment, and i will like to complete my studies, as i was in my 1year in the university when my beloved father died. It is my intention to compensate you with 30% of the total money for your services and the bala nce shall be my capital in your establishment. As soon as I receive your positive response showing your interest I will put things into action immediately. In the light of the above. I shall appreciate an urgent message indicating your ability and willingness to handle this transaction sincerely.

AWAITING YOUR URGENT AND POSITIVE RESPONSE, Please do keep this only to your self for now un till the bank will transfer the fund. I beg you not to disclose it till i come over because I am afraid of my wicked stepmother who has threatened to kill me and have the money alone ,I thank God Today that am out from my country (KENYA) but now In (Burkina Faso) where my father deposited the money with my name as the next of Kin. I have the documents for the claim.

please Reply to this email [preciouskipkalya@xxxxxxcom]
Yours Sincerely
Precious Kipkalya Kones

From: John Kevin Momoh <conney@xxxxxx.ocn.ne.jp>
Date: Thu, Feb 6, 2014 at 9:02 AM
Subject: Call me for more details
To:

Your Urgent Attention;

My Name is John Kevin Momoh (Chief Pilot Virgin Nigeria Airways) I have been trying to reach you on your House delivery address and your telephone about an hour now just to inform you about my successful arrival at JFK International Airport NY USA. With your four boxes of consignment worth $15.5 Million United State Dollars which I have been instructed by the United Nation Head Quarters in Nigeria to be delivered to you.

The Airport authority demanded your contact immediately, so please try and reach me with my world wide diplomatic number (555-555-3933) as I can't afford to spend more time here due to other delivery I have to take care.

I want you to know that you have 24 hours to call me on phone (555-555-3933) as you may know I do not want the security company where this Consignment is lodged to start raising an eye brow because of the length of time it has stayed. However, before the delivery is affected, we need you to reconfirm the following information so that the funds will not be delivered to a wrong person.

1. Full Name
2. Residential Address
3. Direct Telephone Numbers
4. ID passport
5. Age/marital status

After verification of the information with what I have on file, I shall contact you so that we can make arrangements on the exact time I will be bringing your package to your residential address. Send the requested information so that we can proceed.

Regards.

John Kevin Momoh
Chief Pilot Virgin Nigeria Airways
Tel (555-555-3933)
E-mail: john.kvinmomoh72@xxxxxx.com

From: Diplomat Mr. Donald <officedesk7109@xxxxxx.net>
Date: Mon, Feb 10, 2014 at 5:50 AM
Subject: Re: Call me now +15555554380 I just Arrived.
To: imfff12@xxxxxx.com

I am your Diplomat Agent Mr. Wilfred Donald I arrived in (Miami International Air Port) today to deliver your consignment Box worth's $2.5Mlln to you, Call me now +15555554380 or Email me your home Address immediately for me to start coming over to your home. Contact me E-mail; (paul.diplomatjohn@yahoo.fr)

Diplomat: Mr. Wilfred Donald

TONE AND REGISTER

In addition to being formatted correctly and written in language that's free of errors in spelling, grammar, and punctuation, a good business letter has to sound like it's a business letter.

Levels of formality

What makes a business letter sound like a business letter and not like an ordinary letter? Think about that for a minute. Then, read this letter which does not sound very business-like at all:

Subject: Hello

Hi there! Believe me. You're gonna find some very xtra special information in the attachment folder about a special offer from Allied Enterprises. It's gonna change your life. You are adviced to read it very carefully and when you do, I just KNOW ur gonna respond. Hurry: before its too late. Time is running out. You don't wanna miss out on this one. There's no risk! Trust me!!!

Just click here: <link>

Mr Norman Terreli (esquire)
Allied Interprises Inc.

Trust him? Would you trust him enough to click on the link? No one would. That's because there are so many things in Mr. Norman Terreli (esquire)'s letter that would make a reader suspicious about his intentions. Can you spot them? Read the letter again, and identify the ways that Mr. Terreli (esquire) fails to sound business-like.

If Mr. Terreli had read the first seven units of this book like you did, he would know that a good business letter starts with a proper subject heading, is addressed to an actual person or company representative, is spellchecked and error-free, avoids unnecessary capital letters, and never begins with something as chatty and informal as *Hi there!* That's too informal for a business letter. Right away, the writer has chosen a greeting from the wrong register, and by doing so established an informal tone that says, "I'm not serious about business."

Register refers to levels of formality in writing. We determine what register to use by thinking about our purpose for writing and the intended audience. Then, based on this, we choose words and phrases that fit our purpose and won't cause our intended readers to feel upset, offended, or suspicious. In more formal situations, like most business contexts, we write in a formal, polite register. With friends and peers, we usually use an informal, less polite register.

Consider these sentences:

1. We would appreciate it if you would tell your friends about this book.

2. We'd be pleased if you let your friends know about this book.

3. Would you please tell your friends about this book?

4. Please tell your friends about this book.

5. Tell your friends about this book, ok?

Although the primary message is exactly the same in all five sentences, the register is not the same at all. The first sentence is written in a very formal, polite register. The second, third, and fourth sentences are written in increasingly less formal and polite registers. The fifth sentence sounds almost threatening.

This leads us to the matter of tone, which refers to the way writers present themselves. Tone is determined not only by the words chosen, but also by the way they are arranged; and, while more difficult to describe, it is often tone that influences our opinion of the writer, which in turn helps us decide how we feel about the writer's message – and whether we want to respond to it. We hope that the tone of our writing and the register we're using in this book, for example, give you confidence in our message and information, while also making you feel happy about having read this far in the company of friendly, good-natured authors.

Mr. Norman Terreli (esquire) hasn't thought about register or tone at all, and so comes off sounding like a sneaky junior high school student with a nasty secret hidden in his link. That's not how he wants us to think of him. He wants us to think of him as a successful businessman with a wonderful offer that's just a click away.

How could we help him get this message across? Let's start by getting rid of that "Hi there", which we'll replace with:

> Dear (name),

Now, consider these edited versions of Mr. Terreli's opening sentences. As you do, mentally put them in order from the one written in the most formal register and appropriate tone to the one that is the most informal with the least appropriate tone.

1. Here's a special offer from Allied Enterprises. Believe me, it's going to change your life in amazing ways. Don't hesitate to click on the secure link to take advantage of this opportunity. This is something you won't want to miss out on.

2. I'm writing to let you know about a special time-limited offer from Allied Enterprises. As this is an offer which I believe could change your life, I encourage you to read on for more information before following up by registering at our secure company website.

3. This special offer from Allied Enterprises is unbelievable. It's such a life-changer that I know you won't wanna miss out. Just read on for more info. Then click the link and let's get this party started! Trust me, this thing is risk-free.

What do you think?

If you chose the second version as being written in the highest register with the most appropriate tone, you're right. Notice the common phrases often included in most business letters in this version. Also notice the longer sentences, the relative clauses, and the more formal words the writer uses.

> I'm writing to let you know about a special time-limited offer from Allied Enterprises. As this is an offer which I believe could change your life, I encourage you to read on for more information before following up by registering at our secure company website.

We're still not going to click on that link, though.

The first version isn't bad, but notice the things that make it a bit less formal: the shorter sentences, the chattier tone, and the abrupt beginning:

> Here's a special offer from Allied Enterprises. Believe me, it's going to change your life in amazing ways. Don't hesitate to click on the secure link to take advantage of this opportunity. This is something you won't want to miss out on.

In the last version, both the tone and the register are all wrong for a business letter. Notice how abbreviations like *info*, the use of *wanna* instead of *want to*, and informal language like *let's get this party started* (as well as the exclamation point) affect the register and the tone.

> This special offer from Allied Enterprises is unbelievable. It's such a life-changer that I know you won't wanna miss out. Just read on for more info. Then, click the link and let's get this party started! Trust me: this thing is risk-free.

Probably at this point you're thinking, "OK, I've got it"; but still, let's establish a few register and tone rules for you to follow.

When writing business letters:

1. Avoid abbreviations unless they are extremely common, such as UK for United Kingdom or VAT for value-added tax. For example: write *introduction*. Not *intro*. Write *extra*, not *xtra*. Write *great*. Not *gr8t*. You get the idea.

2. Never, ever use *wanna* or *gonna*. These are the reduced speech forms of *want to* and *going to*. *Wanna* and *gonna* and similar reductions like this are never written out – except maybe in chat messages to friends.

3. Make good use of formal phrases and sentences that are common in business letters. Refer back to Unit 6 in this book for examples.

4. Avoid using informal words or phrases. For example, if something tastes good, write that it's *delicious*. Don't write that it's *yummy*. If something is special or unique, use words like that. Don't write that something is *awesome* or *really chill*.

5. If you're not a native speaker of English and aren't sure if your tone and register are right, get someone to read over your letter. If you don't know how to get started, search on the Internet for samples of the kind of business letter you're writing.

6. Don't be a Mr. Norman Terreli and expect that anyone is going to click on your link or open your attachment. Request that recipients reply to get more information. Then, write back with that link or attachment.

WALL OF SHAME

From: Internet Scam Investigation Dept <binbon@xxxxxx.net>
Date: Sat, Feb 1, 2014 at 2:26 PM
Subject: YOUR TRUE FUND INVESTIGATED

ECONOMICAL AND FINANCIAL CRIME COMMISSION
Address:6A Olumeni Street Old GRA,
Port Harcourt, Rivers State

Attention to you,

When your name appeared on the list of approved beneficiaries sometime ago and was submitted here to us, we contacted you to refer you to the Federal Ministry for Finance to seek compensation fund which many received, the email we sent you may have not been delivered or you ignored it, I am writing you now because you are needed to take a decision on the compensation fund you have here, you may have received emails hundreds of emails from impostors in the last few years till date telling you about this and that millions and if you don't come down to Nigeria in person to pursue the release of the ONLY true compensation fund you have here, it will be difficult for you to believe even what I write, the scam you suffered in the past and that experience may even be what will deny you your true fund because once you are scammed you suspect everyone is lying to you and not trustworthy and that is why you are needed here in person or if you do not wish claim the fund, you are needed to confirm you are forfeiting the fund so they can change the ownership of the fund and award to other scammed victims seeking compensation fund.

You need to contact the Foreign Affairs Commission to make inquiry about your true approved fund and the status of that fund, contact the Foreign Affairs Commission, contact Hon Tijani Suleiman on the following email:

Foreign Affairs Commission
Hon Tijani Suleiman
E-mail: info01@xxxxxx.at.pn

For any email you have received telling you about any millions approved here is scammed has been scam perpetrated by impostors, I can go through the records over and over again and tell you there is no other compensation apart from the approved in your name years ago but has been HELD by the FEDERAL MINISTRY FOR FINANCE UNDER ORDERS OF THE FEDERAL GOVERNMENT,you have the chance to claim the fund now and your attention is needed by the Federal Ministry for Finance or if you do not wish to pursue the release of the fund, your confirmation is needed and today.

Waiting for your response.

Detective Alex J.Scott
INTERNET SCAM INVESTIGATION DEPT OF THE Economical and Financial Crime

Unit 8 Exercises

1. List at least five things in this letter that give it an unbusiness-like register and inappropriate tone.

> Subject line: Reply if interested
>
> Hello. I'll skip the intro and get right to the point: A customer died & his fund ($15.2M) is gonna go unclaimed at the bank where I work unless u help me. With the documents at my disposal, I can guide u to receive the $15.2M without any breach of the law. This is for our mutual benefit. Reply if interested.

2. Rewrite the following letter in a more appropriate register with a more formal tone.

> Hey there! Use ur experience and talent and enroll in a premium business manager position at American Dollar and Silver Coins company. American Dollar and Silver Coins Investment Department is on the look our for active peeps who wanna get well-paid work. Let me lay it out for you. American Dollar and Silver Coins is searching for some awesome employees. It's all about rendering services to our customers and our company employees in the USA & also worldwide. We're gonna provide you with all the info you need when hiring you and during your probation period. You've only gotta work about 3-4 hour a day from Monday till Friday. How cool is that? Hit us up for more details. We'll be waiting.

3. Write a short, formal business letter to your teacher or someone who might benefit from using this book. In the letter, recommend this book and then invite the reader to learn more about the company that publishes this book, Wayzgoose Press. Encourage the reader to investigate further by clicking on the company website.

See possible answers and suggested rewrites at the back of the book.

FINAL EXAM

There are two levels of this final exam. You may take one form or both (or consult with your instructor if you are using this textbook in a class).

Form 1: Identify and explain at least five different types of mistakes in each of the letters below. Consider formatting, openings and closings, punctuation, spelling, grammar, topics, and tone.

Form 2: Rewrite one of the letters below to be as correct and appropriate as you can. You may add information as necessary.

1. Letter A

> Dear Zemach
>
> How are you an your family hope all is well,
>
> Yes Let me begin by introducing myself properly to you,I am Aboutrika hamza the personal attorney to Late Engineer P.E. Zemach.who died in auto crash,I am contacting you to put claim on his left deposit of (10.5million dollars) and (GOLD) as the next of kin, with one of the leading Finance Company here in Africa.
>
> Since his death nobody have show up to claim the deposit.So I seek your consent to present you as the next of kin so that the deposit can be release to you since you ber the some last name with late Engineer P.E. Zemach.
>
> The bank has issued me a notice to provide the next of kin, Please do reply with the following information for further clarifications.
>
> Your phone Tel........... You're Fax .... Your Private Email........
>
> I look forward to hearing ayou as soon as possible if you are willing to proceed with me.Reply in my email(aboutrikahamza12@gmail.com)for more details informetion.you can call +228 9014 4960
>
> Respectfully, Aboutrika hamza. Address: #142 Rue du Ankanfu, Lome-Togo Email(aboutrikahamza12@xxxxxx.com)

2. Letter B

UNITED NATIONS OFFICE OF INTERNATIONAL OVERSIGHT SERVICES
INTERNAL AUDIT, MONITORING, CONSULTING AND INVESTIGATIONS DIVISION

MRS MARY MOHAMED

(ATTENTION: PLEASE)

THIS THIS IS TO INFORM YOU THAT I CAME TO BENIN REPUBLIC YESTERDAY
FROM NEW YORK, AFTER SERIES OF MEETINGS WITH US PRESIDENT BARACK
OBAMA, WORLD BANK PRESIDENT ROBERT B. ZOELLICK AND THE UN SECRETARY
GENERAL BAN KI-MOON DUE TO NUMEROUS COMPLAINS FROM
THE FBI AND OTHER SECURITY AGENCIES FROM ASIA, EUROPE, OCEANIA,
ANTARCTICA,SOUTH AMERICA AND THE UNITED STATES OF AMERICA
RESPECTIVELY, AGAINST THE BENIN GOVERNMENT OVER THE RATE OF SCAM/
FRAUDULENT ACTIVITIES GOING ON IN HER COUNTRY.

I HAVE MET WITH THE BENIN NEWLY INSTALLED PRESIDENT OF FEDERAL
REPUBLIC OF BENIN DR YAYI BONII WHO CLAIMED IGNORANT OF THE EVIL
PAPERATED IN HIS COUNTRY BUT PROMISED TO MAKE SURE THAT ALL FUND
BENEFICIARIES/ CONTRACTORS RECEIVE THEIR FUNDS IN THEIR ACCOUNTS
WITHIN NEXT 48HRS. RIGHT NOW, AS DIRECTED IN THE MEETING, WE HAVE
APPROVED A COMPENSATION/PART- PAYMENT OF $2.5M TO ALL AFFECTED
BENEFICIARIES WHICH YOU ARE AMONG. ACCORDINGLY,

WE HAVE WAIVED AWAY ALL YOUR CLEARANCE FEES AND AUTHORIZED THE
GOVERNMENT OF BENIN REPUBLIC TO RELEASE THIS APPROVED FUND TO
YOU WITHOUT ANY DELAY TODAY. THE ONLY FEE YOU WILL PAY TO CONFIRM YOUR
FUND IN YOUR POSSESSION IS YOUR NOTARIZATION FEE TO THE UN IS SUM OF
$48 ONLY.

SO BE ADVICE TO CONTACT ME IMMEDIATELY YOU GET THIS EMAIL NOW BECAUSE
EVERY THING HAS BEEN DONE OK.AND FOR YOUR INFORMATION

ONCE AGAIN NOTE: THAT THIS IS NOT ONE OF THOSE NIGERIAN / BENIN AFRICAN
SCAMS THAT ALL THEY ARE AFTER IS TO RIPE YOU OFF YOUR MONEY AND AT THE
END YOU WILL NOT RECEIVE YOUR FUNDS, BUT NOTE THAT THIS IS NO SCAM AND
IS DIRECTLY FROM OUR PRESIDENT BARACK OBAMA.

ONCE YOU SEND THE MONEY, TRY TO NOTIFY ME WITH THE MTCN FOR EASY PICK UP AND FOR IMMEDIATE ACTION ON THE RELEASE OF YOUR FUNDS,FOR EASIER RECEIVE OF YOUR INHERITED FUNDS WITHOUT ANY FURTHER DELAY. SINCE YOU WAS UNABLE TO RECEIVE YOUR PAYMENT OF $10.000 MTCN THROUGH WESTERN UNION DUE TO THEIR MANAGEMENT FOR FULL COMPENSATION PAYMENT OF $2.500.000.00USD

RECEIVERS NAME:NWAKASI NNADMDI
COUNTRY: BENIN REPUBLIC
CITY COTONOU
CODE: 229
TEST QUESTION: TRUST
ANSWER: RELIVE
AMOUNT: $48 ONLY

I HAVE A VERY LIMITED TIME TO STAY IN BENIN REPUBLIC HERE SO I WOULD LIKE YOU TO URGENTLY RESPOND TO THIS MESSAGE FOR MORE DIRECTIVES. FOR ORAL DISCUSSION, CALL ME ON THIS NUMBER WHICH I JUST ACQUIRED IN YESTERDAY:+229

SINCERELY YOURS,
MRS MARY MOHAMED
UNITED NATIONS UNDER-SECRETARY
GENERAL FOR INTERNAL

ANSWER KEY

Unit 1: Formatting (page 10)

1. Possible answers:

   a. There is no greeting or closing. Or paragraphs. Or sentences! Many mistakes with capital letters.

   b. There is no greeting. The letter is in light gray letters, not black. There are mistakes in capitalization and spacing.

2. Possible answers:

   Following conventions helps your reader easily understand what you are trying to communicate. It shows that you are a member of the business community, and that you understand how business is conducted and can behave appropriately. That makes you seem more trustworthy.

Unit 2: Openings and Closings (page 18)

Sample answers:

1.

> Dear Mr. Umbro,
>
> I'd appreciate it if you'd take a moment to have a look at our new singles site.
>
> Sincerely,
>
> Elena Ludmila

2.

> Dear Mr. Sandy,
>
> I'm doing some research about motivation. I understand this is an area that you have also done some research in, and I'm hoping that you could direct me to some good resources on the Internet.
>
> Best wishes,
>
> Adi Cerman

3.

> To Whom It May Concern:
>
> I would like to inform you that there is an error in my recent bill. Could you please check the attached copy against your records and correct the error as soon as possible? My account number is A111223334. Thank you.
>
> Sincerely,
>
> Jennifer Lorant

4.

> Dear Ms. Zemach,
>
> As you know, I have a package for you that I would like to deliver. However, I need to get your current contact information and know how best to meet you near the Portland International Airport.
>
> My flight is this coming Thursday, so I need to hear from you before I fly. If you do not get back to me before then, I cannot accept responsibility for failing to deliver this package to you in a timely manner.
>
> Sincerely,
>
> Ambassador Terrance McCuley
> US Embassy
> Abuja, Nigeria

5.

> Dear Mr. Wilson,
>
> It has come to my attention that we will be unable to deliver the full amount of $3.7 million dollars to you via Western Union. The maximum amount that Western Union allows to be transferred on any given day is $5000. Given this, I will begin transferring $5000 per day into your account and will continue doing so until you receive the entire $3.7 million dollars. I trust that this is acceptable.
>
> Please reply at your earliest convenience.
>
> Sincerely,
>
> Douglas Hall
> Email: Douglashall2006@xxxxxx.in.th
> Phone: +555 99-36-35

Unit 3: Punctuation and Capitalization (page 27)

(Note that the corrections are *only* for punctuation and capitalization, and not grammar, tone, or topic.)

1.

> Dear Chuck,
>
> How are you? I hope all is OK! My name is Tayna. I'm a rather shy girl at first, but I open up a little more as I get to know someone. I attach my photo. I hope you like it. I am not a clever girl, but I am kind. I like craftwork, baking, sewing, and so on. I do many things to make myself happy; for example, playing piano, dancing to music, doing aerobics, and listening to stories. I am looking for a strong, decent man. I do not know what to write because I never used the Internet for acquaintance before.
>
> Write to me if you want to learn more about me and see my other pictures. I will wait your letter. Write to me soon. I will send another photo.
>
> Take care,
>
> Tanya
> P.S. There is a chance we can do the business also.

2.

> If your bank immediately closes your account, the funds will bounce back to us. When we receive the funds, we will automatically deposit them to the verified bank account on file. Once this happens, you will have three days to contact us, give us your information, and tell us what to do with your funds.
>
> Kaw Valley State Bank

3.

> Hello Mr. Sandy,
>
> Are you ready to find out anything? This confidential software is something they want banned in all 50 states. This is because these secrets were never intended to reach your eyes. With this software, you can get facts on anyone using the Internet. You will be able to locate missing persons, find lost relatives, obtain the addresses and phone numbers of old school friends, and even skip trace deadbeat spouses. This is not a private investigator, but rather a sophisticated software program with links to thousands of public record bases, designed to automatically crack your case.

4.

> Dear Mr. Sandy,
>
> My name is Trevor Emmanuel.

5.

> Remember to send them your current information:
>
> Your full name:
>
> Your home address:
>
> Your home phone number:
>
> Your cell phone number:
>
> Your personal identification:

Unit 4: Spelling (page 33)

1. payment
2. throat
3. below (*bellow* is a word, but it means "yell" and not "under." *Demurrage* is not a common English word – but it is a word!)
4. forty
5. lose (*loose* is an adjective, and a verb is needed in that sentence)
6. prove
7. university; degree; doctorate; bachelor's; doctorate (yes, they misspelled it twice)
8. any further (must be two words); communication; fraudster

Unit 5: Grammar (page 39)

1. b
2. a
3. a
4. b
5. b

6.

> For your information, I have paid the delivery charge, insurance premium, and clearance certificate fees of the cheque to show that it is not drug money or meant to sponsor a terrorist attack in your country.

(Note that *cheque* is a British English spelling; in American English, it would be *check*. But *cheque* is not wrong.)

7.

> Remember, I was supposed to have traveled last week, but the weather was too bad. I will be leaving for Paraguay tomorrow.

Unit 6: Common Expressions (page 47)

1. Some other ways Mr. Dennis could make his letter more business-like and more believable include:

- Going into more detail in the letter itself rather than attaching a document.
- Coming up with a story that doesn't involve a famous person and millions of dollars that can be had for little effort. Life doesn't work that way.
- Sending his mail from a business-like address.
- Including a logo from the Bank of Nigeria following his signature

2. Possible answer:

Dear Mr. Sandy,

Although I had been authorized to transfer 8.5 million US dollars into your account to complete a contractual agreement, something has come up that is now preventing me from proceeding with this transaction.

Mrs. Virgie Brown has recently contacted us claiming that you have passed away, and that she is now entitled to this money as she is your next of kin. Still, although we have searched available records, we can find no notice of your death. If you are indeed alive, could you please contact me as soon as possible with your contact information? Once I receive your confirmation, I will be able to release these funds to you.

Please accept my apologies for this intrusion now and for the long delay in contacting you about this matter. As you can imagine, it's a complicated situation. Still, I am aware that this payment to you is long overdue, and for this I also apologize.

I do hope you are alive and that you'll be able to reply to this letter promptly.

Sincerely,
Nathan Oosthuizen
International Monetary Fund Head Office
Washington, DC

Unit 7: Appropriate Topics (page 54)

1. a, b, c, d, e, f, g, h, i, j, k, l

2. Possible answers:

Letter A

> Inappropriate greeting, sentences with no end punctuation, inappropriate topics (including injury and personal hard luck stories), missing spaces between words, missing apostrophe in *lets*, improper capitalization of *lawyer*, no comma after the closing, an extra period after the signature, the urging to keep the letter secret, and more.

Letter B

> Missing name in greeting, inappropriate topics (call to pity), first person pronoun I not capitalized, sentences not ended with periods, too much detail about deceased family members, link to outside information, incorrect capitalization (*Country*, *Father*, *File*, and more), grammatical and spelling mistakes (*convince Ed* instead of *convinced*), some words in all capital letters (AWAITING YOUR URGENT etc.), no comma after the closing, and more.

Unit 8: Tone and Register (page 64)

1. Some of the things which put the letter in an unbusiness-like register and give it an inappropriate tone:

- The inappropriate subject heading
- Not addressing the letter to a person
- Beginning with an informal greeting
- Using abbreviations like *intro*
- Writing *u* for *you*
- Using *gonna* instead of *going* to
- Using an informal phrase like *I'll skip the intro and get right to the point*
- Not concluding the letter with a proper business-like phrase
- Not using an appropriate closing or signing the letter

2. Possible answers:

Dear Ms. Zemach,

I'm writing today to tell you about an exciting employment opportunity with the American Dollar and Silver Coins Company.

We're currently seeking motivated, energetic people to apply for a position as business manager in our Investment Department and would like to encourage you to apply. This is a well-paid position that involves rendering services to our customers and employees in the United States and in our worldwide network. The work only takes three to four hours per day, and you'll of course have your weekends free. I'll provide you with all the details you'll need to apply for this position when you reply. Upon being hired, you'll then go through a training program for which you'll be paid.

Please reply as soon as possible, so that I can walk you through the application and hiring process.

I'm looking forward to hearing from you.

Sincerely,

Chuck Sandy
Director of Employment

Final Exam (page 65)

1. Letter A

Form 1:

Incorrect opening (no title before Zemach), no question mark at the end of the first sentence, non-relevant topic (asking about family), sender's surname in the first paragraph is not capitalized, there are no spaces between several sentences, the word "gold" is all in capital letters… and many more.

Form 2: Possible answers:

Dear Ms. Zemach,

I am the personal attorney to P.E. Zemach, who died recently in a car accident. I am contacting you about his estate in case you are his next of kin.

The bank would like the following information to determine if you will inherit from Mr. Zemach.

Telephone number:
Fax:
Email:

I look forward to hearing from you as soon as possible. Please reply by email or by phone at +555-9014-4960.

Respectfully,
Aboutrika Hamza

#142 Rue du Ankanfu
Lome, Togo
aboutrikahamza12@xxxxxx.com.

2. Letter B

Form 1:

The letter is written in all capital letters, there is no proper greeting, there are repeated words (THIS THIS), incorrect word forms are used (*advice* for *advise*), the phone number is incomplete, and many more.

Form 2: Possible answers:

> Dear Mr. Sandy,
>
> I am writing to inform you that I have just come from a series of meetings with U.S. President Barack Obama, World Bank President Robert B. Zoellick, and UN Secretary Ban Ki-Moon about complaints from the FBI and other security agencies around the world against the government of Benin in regards to fraudulent activities.
>
> President Yayi Bonii of Benin has promised that all fund beneficiaries and contractors will receive their funds in their accounts within the next 48 hours. A compensation partial payment of $2.5 million will be paid to all affected beneficiaries, of which you are one.
>
> We have waived all clearance fees and authorized the government of Benin to release these approved funds to you without any further delay. The only fee you must pay is the notarization fee to the UN of US$48.
>
> Please send this amount by Western Union.
>
> Receiver's Name: Nwakasi Nnadmdi
> Country: Benin
> City: Cotonou
> Code: 229
> Test question: Trust
> Answer: Relive
> Amount: $48
>
> Please contact me as soon as you get this email.
>
> Sincerely yours,
> Mary Mohamed
>
> United Nations Under-Secretary General for Internal Affairs
> United Nations Office of International Oversight Services
> Internal Audit, Monitoring, Consulting, and Investigations Division

From: Barrister Mark Ferguson <info@xxxxxx.com>
Date: Tue, Feb 4, 2014 at 2:01 PM
Subject: Your prompt response is highly imperative
To: Recipients <info@xxxxxx.com>

From: Barrister Mark Ferguson
Chambers & Advocates
Address: 60 Bayswater Road
London W2 3PS, United Kingdom
Tel: +555-9374-19300
Fax: +555-8704-46063

Good day.
I am sorry for contacting you through this medium without a previous notice; I had to use email because it is an official and more confidential way of making contact with people around the world. My names are Mark Ferguson a fifty three (53) years old Attorney in practice here in London. I had a client by name Michelangelo Manini who is an Italian and producer of electronic gates based in Italy who died on March 17 2012 at the age of 50.Prior to the Death of my Late Client, He secured a contract of 22,500,000.00 million Pounds from the British Airways, following which he received a 30% mobilization fee of 6,750,000.00 Million Pounds and successfully executed the contract, but the balance of 15,750,000.00 Million Pounds contract payment was in the Process of being transferred into My Late Client's account with BARCLAY`S BANK London which he submitted to the British Airways before he lost his life in the incidence.

Just one week after this sudden Death, The British Airways affected the transfer of the balance of his Contract funds into the account that my late client has on his file with them. As one of his personal attorney here in London United Kingdom after his death I have been officially notified and instructed by the BARCLAY`S BANK London where the money is currently deposited that I should provide and forward the particulars of Mr. Michelangelo next of kin so that the funds in his account can be remitted into his next of Kin's account in accordance with British Laws. However, as the personal attorney and close confident of late Mr. Michelangelo, I want you to know that my late Client died intestate, He died without leaving a next of kin for this particular will stated, we are to transfer this funds from the BARCLAY`S BANK London as soon as possible before Andrea Moschetti, the lawyer appointed by the Catholic Church could discover about this will.

Therefore I am seeking for your consent to present you as the deceased next of kin and subsequently the beneficiary of the fund so that the proceed of this account valued at 15,750,000.00 Million Pounds can be paid to you for subsequent disbursement between you and I.If you can cooperate with me and receive these funds as next of kin to late Mr. Michelangelo Manini, Confirm your interest by contacting me through my confidential email above. I can assure you that the deal is 100% risk free because I am in possession of the deceased personal file which contains all information which I shall use to prove your relationship with the deceased therefore the money will be paid into the account of whomever I present as LATE Mr. Michelangelo Manini Next of kin with proofs that I will present to the bank when needed, we would both share in ratio of 60% for me and 40% for you, am giving you 40% from the total funds due to it matter of urgency.

When I receive a positive response and after proper discussion with you, I will furnish you all relevant information that will facilitate the release of the Funds to you. An application will have to be filed to the bank for processing of the release of the funds into your nominated Bank account anywhere in the world. please kindly send to me your full name, address, mobile number and fax for easy communication and do reply me through my private email address:(barr_markferguson@xxxxxx.com)for more information's. Hope to hear from you through the above e-mail address .Your prompt response is highly imperative.

Yours truly,
Barrister Mark Ferguson

ABOUT THE AUTHORS

Chuck Sandy is a teacher, teacher trainer, author, and educational activist with 30 years of experience. His many publications include the *Passages* and *Connect* series from Cambridge University Press and the *Active Skills For Communication* series from Cengage Learning. He is a frequent presenter at conferences and workshops around the world, and is a cofounder and director of the International Teacher Development Institute (iTDi). Chuck believes that positive change in education happens one student, one classroom, and one school at a time, and that it arises most readily out of dialogue and in collaboration with other educators. This is the reason he has worked to spread Design For Change across the world and why he's become so devoted to the mission that drives http://iTDi.pro : to make professional teacher development accessible and affordable for all teachers. His blog posts about education can be found at http://itdi.pro/blog/author/chuck/.

Dorothy E. Zemach taught English, French, and Japanese for over 18 years in Asia, Africa, and the US. She holds an MA in TESL from the School for International Training in Vermont, USA. Now she concentrates on writing and editing English language teaching materials and textbooks and conducting teacher training workshops. Her areas of specialty and interest are teaching writing, teaching reading, business English, academic English, testing, and humor.

Her writing textbooks include *Writers at Work: The Essay* (Cambridge University Press), *Writing Sentences, Writing Paragraphs, Writing Essays,* and *Writing Research Papers* (Macmillan), and *Writing Power*, levels 3 and 4 (Pearson).

She is a frequent plenary speaker at international conferences, and a regular blogger for Teacher Talk at http://azargrammar.com.

In 2012, Dorothy launched Wayzgoose Press to publish quality works of fiction and non-fiction.

She does not have esophageal cancer.

www.ingramcontent.com/pod-product-compliance
Lightning Source LLC
Chambersburg PA
CBHW042015080426
42735CB00002B/66